TABLE TALK

TOUGH QUESTIONS
QUICK ANSWERS

Arthur E. Helft, M.D.

Published 2009 by Arthur E. Helft, M.D.

To my children
Joseph, Ayala, Steven, Malka, Will, Shari,
Josh and Susie
and to my wife Rifki
whose table talk inspired this compilation

PREFACE

It has been my impression that when friends get together at dinner or on social occasions, discussions usually turn to sports, contemporary news events, gossip, or the weather. This is not because most people are incapable of considering serious issues, but these issues are not usually foremost in peoples' minds. The purpose of this book is to present a number of serious ethical, medical, social, and legal issues about which there is understandable disagreement.

These issues have interested me, and hopefully will interest the readers of this book. My family and I have discussed current controversial issues over dinner and lively discussions have ensued. Family and friends have enthusiastically suggested other topics for discussion. Questions are raised and brief pros and cons are given. There are no right or wrong answers. By presenting these issues everyone is given an opportunity to think about these problems and formulate and present his or her own opinion.

Hopefully, you will enjoy discussing these issues as much as I have enjoyed editing this book. My family has had great table talk, and I hope you will too. You may contact the author with any comments, suggestions, or questions at aehelft@gmail.com.

The first edition of this book was published in 2006 and was very well received. Since that time, I have added another thirty five topics worthy of discussion. In addition, multiple *Related Issues* have been added. I hope that you continue to use and enjoy the book.

TABLE OF CONTENTS

LAW AND ORDER

SEX IN THE CITY

TO YOUR HEALTH

FAITH MATTERS

SCHOOLS AND RULES

WATCH WHAT YOU SAY

POTPOURRI

Q Should gambling be legalized?

While casino gambling is illegal in New York State, the State's lottery jackpot hit 13 million dollars, and the State encourages citizens to purchase lottery tickets.

Should lotteries, casino gambling, and off track betting be promoted by the State?

Yes:
- ✓ Gambling provides diversion and pleasure for millions of people.
- ✓ No one is forced to gamble and people should be free to decide if they want to gamble or not.
- ✓ Legalized gambling provides income to the State and promotes tourism.

No:
- Legalizing gambling creates gambling addicts, and increases the demand for gambling by people who can ill afford it.
- Gambling entices poor people with the unrealistic hope of attaining instant riches.
- Gambling attracts racketeers and mobsters and increases crime from victims trying to recoup gambling losses.
- Gambling weakens the stability of family life, increases divorce and wrecks lives.
- Lottery revenues often replace rather than supplement legislative appropriations.
- Gambling "enriches the few and impoverishes the many."

# Q

Should internet gambling be allowed?

While gambling is prohibited in New York, many New Yorker's are wagering on an internet web site operated by World Sports Exchange, located on the Island of Antigua, where gambling is allowed. Consumer demand and the States' desire for further revenues are increasing the pressure for legalization.

Should such gambling be allowed?

Yes:

- ✓ Americans love to gamble and gambling is a source of pleasure for millions of people.
- ✓ Prohibiting internet gambling would be impossible to enforce as we do not have legal jurisdiction over people abroad who are organizing such web sites in countries where they are legal.
- ✓ Outlawing internet gambling domestically will simply push the business overseas.
- ✓ Few Americans regard gambling as immoral.
- ✓ Stock market day trading is perfectly legal, though it too is a form of gambling.
- ✓ Government sponsored lotteries are legal, and governments employ get rich quick marketing techniques to promote gambling.
- ✓ Indian tribes which are allowed to run gambling casinos should be allowed to provide online gambling services.
- ✓ If pornography sites and hate group sites are not banned from the internet, why should gambling sites be banned?
- ✓ Prohibition is a limitation of individual freedom.

No:

- • The internet promotes casual gambling, underage gambling, and credit-based gambling to those who would not ordinarily gamble.
- • Easy access to gambling sites promotes gambling addiction and makes it easier for minors to gamble.

Q. Should the One Child policy for population control be instituted?

In 1979 the Chinese government introduced a policy to overcome the problem of over-population and over-consumption, by allowing only one child per family. Couples who have more than one child are fined and their children may be denied governmental benefits such as access to free education and healthcare. Exceptions have been made for parents of severely disabled or deceased children and for parents who lost children in the recent Sichuan province earthquake. There are probably three to four hundred million fewer Chinese people today because of the one child policy.

Should the government force parents to limit their family to only one child?

Yes:
- ✓ It is good for the country because social and environmental problems are alleviated.
- ✓ Problems associated with over-population, like slums, overextended social services, epidemics, depletion of natural resources, and exploitation of surplus labor are reduced.
- ✓ With fewer children, women have more time to pursue their careers.
- ✓ Many people believe that one child is enough.

No:
- The policy is contrary to the basic human right of reproduction.
- Individuals and not the state should determine family size.
- The policy promotes bribery, forced sterilization, and abortion.
- Because most Chinese families prefer sons, portable ultrasound devices are being used to identify and abort female fetuses.
- Older citizens will be unable to rely on their children to care for them in their old age.
- The free market will solve the over-population problem.
- Wealthy couples can circumvent this law by turning to fertility clinics to initiate multiple births, which are not subject to fines and penalties, as long as it is their first birth.
- An only child may become spoiled because of all the attention lavished upon him or her by both parents.

Related Issue:
Should Nadya Suleman, 33, a single mother of six children receiving welfare payments, have been allowed to deliver octuplets conceived by in vitro fertilization (IVF)?

Should sexual orientation be considered in adoption?

Charles Lofton and his partner Roger Croteau, both nurses, have been foster parents for the past ten years to a baby infected with HIV since birth. Because of a state law which does not allow gay people to adopt children and forbids them to become legal parents, the department of social services wants to transfer the boy from the only father he has known to a heterosexual home.

Should Mr. Lofton be allowed to adopt the boy?

Yes:
- ✓ Most children in the United States do not live in homes with a mother and father who are married, and single parents are allowed to adopt children.
- ✓ Children brought up by gay parents do just as well emotionally and are as successful as those brought up by heterosexuals.
- ✓ Good parenting is not dependent upon sexual orientation.
- ✓ There are many children waiting to be adopted, and older children and those with special needs are hard to place.
- ✓ There is no connection between homosexuality and child sexual abuse.
- ✓ Sexual orientation of parents has no impact on the sexual orientation of their children.

No:
- Children are better off in homes with a married mother and father.
- Children need a mother and father for proper role models.
- Children of gay parents may be ridiculed and rejected by their peers.
- Gays do not have stable relationships and will not provide good parenting.
- Children raised by gay parents are more likely to grow up gay themselves.

Addendum:
The Supreme Court would not hear a challenge to overturn Florida's law banning Gay adoptions. The State of Arkansas in 2008 voted to ban all unmarried couples from adopting or fostering children.

Related Issue:
JL and EH were in a lesbian relationship for ten years. EH was the biological mother of a young child that both women had cared for. After separating, JL filed a request for joint custody, claiming that she was a de facto parent. The biological mom argued that her former partner had no right to petition for custody because of a lack of a legally recognized family relationship.

Q   Should race be considered in adoption?

Intercultural adoptions are adoptions which take place between members of different racial, ethnic, or religious groups. The National Association of Black Social Workers is vehemently opposed to the placement of black children in white foster or adoptive homes. The Multiethnic Placement Act of 1994, requires agencies receiving federal funds to adopt a color blind approach and not deny placement on the basis of race or nationality.

Should intercultural adoptions be allowed?

Yes:
- ✓ Children wait longer in foster care to be adopted when race is allowed to be a consideration.
- ✓ Minority children are a majority of those in foster care awaiting adoption.
- ✓ Early adoption is in the best interest of the child.
- ✓ Most intercultural adopted children are well adjusted and do not develop psychological problems.
- ✓ President Obama is a product of an interracial family.
- ✓ There aren't enough black parents willing to adopt black children.

No:
- • We live in a race-conscious society and intercultural adoption creates identity issues for the child.
- • The child may become socially marginalized.
- • The child might develop psychological problems.
- • White parents are ill prepared for the challenges of raising a child of a different race.
- • A member of one culture cannot be a teacher of another's cultural heritage.

Q

Should a non-biological de facto parent be granted custody privileges?

There are two types of custody - physical custody and legal custody. Physical custody refers to where and with whom the child lives, while legal custody refers to the party who is authorized to make important life decisions for the child, such as which school or which church to attend. Custody may be shared or given to one parent, with the Court basing its decision on what is in the best interest of the child. Most children being raised by lesbians and gay men are adopted, or were conceived during their parents' prior heterosexual relationship before coming out as lesbian or gay, or were conceived by artificial insemination. The degree to which the sexual orientation of a parent is used in determining a custody arrangement varies, depending upon the jurisdiction of the court.

Who should get custody in the following cases?

❖ Lisa Wagner and Kathleen Crandall lived together as domestic partners and jointly decided to have a child. Wagner gave birth to the child by artificial insemination and Crandall's surname was given to the child. When the couple separated after eleven years, Crandall continued to visit regularly with the child with whom she shared a loving relationship. Wagner cut off her former partner's contact with the child and Crandall initiated custody and visitation proceedings.

❖ Joel and Evelyn A. lived together for ten years bringing up their two children ages eight and four. On separation Joel sought custodial privileges even though DNA tests disproved his paternity claim.

❖ In 1966, Jodilynn Jacob and Jennifer Lee Shultz-Jacob entered into a lesbian relationship and in 2002 received a civil-union license in Vermont. Carl Frampton donated sperm to help Schultz-Jacob conceive two children, and he was involved in their lives, and voluntarily contributed to their support. In 2006 Jacob and Shultz-Jacob separated. The three parties were granted partial custody and the Pennsylvania appellate court found that a child can have three parents simultaneously, each liable for child support.

❖ Unable to have children of their own, Amy and Scott Kehoe paid to obtain sperm from a bright and athletic sperm donor in California and to obtain eggs from a pre-med student egg donor in Michigan. They also paid a fertility clinic to perform in vitro fertilization (IVF) and implant the fertilized ova into Laschell Baker who agreed to act as a surrogate mother and carry the embryos to term. In July 2009, twins were born and taken home from the hospital by the Kehoes. One month later, after learning that Ms. Kehoe was being treated for mental illness, Ms. Baker obtained a court order to have the twins returned to her custody. Should custody be granted to the sperm donor, the egg donor, the gestational mother, or the Kehoes? (see page 47)

Q **Should a child of a gay union be entitled to social security survivor benefits?**

❖ Tom and Doris have been married for forty years. Tom dies unexpectedly and Doris is eligible to receive survivor benefits from Social Security. JoAnne and Jane are in the exact same situation. They have been together for forty years but when JoAnne dies, unlike the married widow, Jane cannot benefit from the Social Security system.

❖ Lisa Stewart is a 33-year-old de facto parent who has terminal breast cancer. When she dies she will leave a five-year-old daughter along with her partner of ten years, neither of whom will be entitled to social security survivor benefits.

Q

Should a parent with physical custody of a minor child be allowed to move out of state?

Wendy Burgess of Lancaster, CA, sought to move 40 miles from her ex-husband with whom she had joint custody, to take a better-paying job, but a court ruled that she would lose custody if she did.

Addendum:
On appeal, the California Supreme Court ruled that "it is unrealistic to assume that divorced parents will permanently remain in the same location after dissolution."

Related Issues:
Should sexual orientation be a consideration in determining child custody?
After being married for eight years and having two kids, RH divorces her husband and comes out as a lesbian. She is concerned that her heterosexual husband will obtain custody of their two children, ages six and four.

Theron McGriff and his ex-wife shared joint custody of their two children after their divorce. Three years later, when the children's mother found out that her ex-husband was involved in a relationship with another man, she petitioned the court for sole custody of the children based on the fact that her ex-husband was gay.

Q Should asylum be granted to victims of female genital cutting?

Genital cutting also called female circumcision or female genital mutilation, involves removing or altering a woman's genitalia. It is a very common custom which has long been practiced on young girls in Africa.

Fauziya Kasinga, 19, a native of Togo, is seeking asylum in the United States, claiming that she fled her home in Togo to escape genital cutting customarily performed in her country.

Should Ms. Kasinga be granted asylum in the U.S.?

Yes:
- ✓ The procedure is usually performed with unsterilized instruments or razor blades with no anesthesia, and can cause serious medical complications.
- ✓ The procedure deprives women of a fulfilling sexual life.
- ✓ Genital cutting is a form of sexual oppression, abuse, and persecution.
- ✓ Women's rights should be protected.

No:
- Genital cutting promotes virtue and chastity in women by eliminating sexual satisfaction.
- Granting asylum would open the doors of immigration to millions of potential asylum seekers.
- We should not judge the cultural practices of other countries.

> Addendum:
> Female genital mutilation has been classified by the federal courts as a form of persecution and the U.S. government considers the fear of genital mutilation sufficient cause for granting asylum.

Related Issue:
Should Alima Traore, who was subject to genital mutilation (a form of persecution) and now in the U.S. on a student visa, be deported to her native Mali where her father will force her to marry a first cousin whom she doesn't love and her daughters, should she have any, would be subject to genital mutilation?

The Board of Immigration Appeals rejected Ms. Traore's asylum request, stating that genital mutilation is a one-time procedure and she will therefore not be subject to further persecution. The Board also rejected her forced marriage claim.

Q

Should undocumented immigrants be deported to their country of origin?

An undocumented immigrant is a person who has entered the United States illegally or continues to reside in the country after his visa expires. Immigrants usually leave their country for political reasons (to avoid persecution in their home country) or economic reasons (to better their economic situation). It has been estimated that there are at least 7,500,000 unauthorized workers from Mexico and elsewhere (mostly Central America) working in the U.S. in 2005, with household members totaling about 12 million and increasing at 700,000 to 1,500,000 per year or 2,000 to 5,000 per day. Unauthorized immigrants are able to find work because they can be paid less than the legal minimum wage or have unsafe working conditions. Employer penalties are rarely enforced and forged documents are plentiful. The nation must decide on how many and which immigrants to admit and what to do with the undocumented immigrants already residing in the United States.

Kenneth Harrell, a 35-year-old Assemblies of God pastor in South Carolina, and an American citizen, met and later married Gricelda Molina, a 35-year-old undocumented factory worker from Honduras who had previously been deported for entering the U.S. illegally. After giving birth to two sons and pregnant with their third child, Ms. Molina was deported.

Should undocumented immigrants be deported?

<u>Yes:</u>

- ✓ The presence of unauthorized immigrants results in increased costs for social services and increased crime and unemployment.
- ✓ Unauthorized immigrants bring alien political and social values.
- ✓ Undocumented immigrants do not undergo health screening prior to entry into the United States, and may bring diseases, such as tuberculosis, into the country.
- ✓ Our borders should be more secure in the post 9/11 era.
- ✓ Low skilled Americans suffer from competition with the immigrants.
- ✓ The presence of unauthorized immigrants results in wage and benefit reductions.
- ✓ A barrier should be built along the 2,000 mile border between the U.S. and Mexico.
- ✓ Violators of the law should not be offered amnesty, as amnesty rewards law breaking.
- ✓ Sham marriages are arranged in an attempt to obtain legal status.

Q Should undocumented immigrants be deported to their country of origin?

No:

- Immigrants fill jobs that Americans won't take.
- Taxes paid by immigrants cover the costs of their social services.
- Undocumented immigrants are necessary to keep production costs low and allow American corporations to compete in the global economy.
- Businesses require a steady stream of cheap labor.
- We cannot deport 12 million people.
- Immigrants should be admitted to the U.S. as temporary workers.
- We are a nation of immigrants.
- The government should not separate families.

Related Issue:
The city of Hazleton, PA, passed the Illegal Immigration Relief Act, which made English the city's official language, and fined those who hired or rented to undocumented immigrants. The ACLU of PA challenged the ordinance which forbids illegal immigrants from renting property and requires city documents to be printed only in English.

Addendum:
In July 2007, federal Judge James Munley ruled that immigration is a national issue, and he struck down Hazleton's city ordinance.

Related Issue:
Saida Umanzor, 26, originally from Honduras, was arrested after immigration agents determined that she had been ordered deported in July 2006, after missing an immigration court hearing. Ms. Umanzor was with two of her United States born children, 9-month-old Brittney whom she was breast feeding, and 3-year-old Alexandra. Under the 14th Amendment, any child born in the U.S. is a citizen and cannot be deported. Saida and her husband, also an undocumented immigrant, are being forced to return to Honduras with no job and no money, penalizing their American born children.

Other Issues for Consideration:
Should undocumented immigrants be allowed to obtain a driver's license?

Should undocumented immigrants be allowed to attend public schools?

Should undocumented immigrants be allowed to obtain free municipal health care or food stamps?

11

Q

Should U.S. citizens have the right to own a gun?

The Second Amendment to the Constitution states: "A well regulated militia, being necessary to the security of a free state, the right of the people to keep and bear arms, shall not be infringed." Dick Heller, a security guard, sued the District of Columbia, after it denied him permission to register and keep a handgun for self-defense within his home. He claimed that the district's ban on handgun ownership violated his Second Amendment rights

Should Mr. Heller be allowed to keep a gun in his home?

Yes:
- ✓ Individual self defense and gun ownership is a right guaranteed by the Constitution.
- ✓ Banning guns does not make communities safer, just the opposite, gun bans create guaranteed victims.
- ✓ Gun bans are ineffective and create an active black market.
- ✓ Gun restrictions reduce suicide and homicide by guns, but without any net decline in deaths because of substitution of other methods of assault.
- ✓ Gun ownership within the general population hinders the establishment of totalitarian control.
- ✓ Gun purchases are subject to licensing restrictions. One must be over twenty one and have no criminal record in order to purchase a gun.
- ✓ Allowing citizens to carry guns deters crime, because criminals do not know who may or may not be carrying a firearm.

No:
- There is a problem of handgun violence in the United States.
- Handguns are involved in numerous accidental deaths, murders, suicides, assaults, and robberies. Their absence will reduce the level of violent crimes.
- The handgun ban is an important public safety measure.
- More Americans are killed, particularly in congested crime-ridden urban areas, because of the easy availability of guns.
- The risk of a domestic dispute or a volatile situation resulting in a fatality is much higher when a gun is readily available.
- The right to freedom from assault outweighs the right to bear arms.

Should U.S. citizens have the right to own a gun?

Addendum:

The Supreme Court in June 2008 declared that the Second Amendment allows an individual to own a gun for self-defense. The Court rejected the view that "the right of the people to keep and bear arms" applies only in connection with service in "a well regulated militia."

The regulation of guns, as opposed to their banning is permissible, and prohibitions on the possession of firearms by felons and the mentally ill, or laws forbidding the carrying of firearms in sensitive places such as schools and government buildings remain operative.

Related Issue:

Should the city of San Francisco continue to ban handguns in public housing? San Francisco has 12,000 residents living in public housing, who are required to sign a lease that forbids weapon possession under the penalty of eviction.

Related Issue:

Should a rural Texas school district continue to allow some teachers, after special training, to carry concealed weapons in order to provide improved security for its students and possibly another Columbine High School tragedy? (See page 87)

Q Should the death penalty be abolished?

John Smith was found guilty of killing a bank guard during a holdup and was sentenced to death by lethal injection. His lawyer claims that the death penalty is cruel and unusual punishment.

Should the death penalty be abolished?

Yes:
- ✓ Capital punishment does not act as a deterrent to others.
- ✓ Many mistakenly convicted death row prisoners have been freed in recent years.
- ✓ The death penalty is not applied in an even manner around the country.
- ✓ Death row inmates frequently have poor legal representation.
- ✓ There are frequently mitigating circumstances such as psychological problems or an abusive childhood, and murderers may not be fully accountable for their actions.

No:
- Capital punishment acts as a deterrent to others.
- We should abide by the principle of a life for a life.
- The death penalty should be continued, but conviction should be based not on evidence beyond a reasonable doubt, but upon evidence beyond any doubt.
- Families of victims receive some sort of solace from retribution.
- Mitigating circumstances are always taken into consideration.

Q Should elderly inmates be paroled?

Dr. Charles Friedgood, a Long Island surgeon, was convicted in 1977 of murdering his wife. He tried to embezzle several hundred thousand dollars from his wife's estate and planned to fly to Europe to join a Danish nurse with whom he had fathered two children. He was sentenced to 25 years to life in prison and now at age 89, he has served over twenty five years in prison, and is New York State's oldest prison inmate. He has requested a parole from the New York State Parole Board which had denied his request on multiple prior occasions.

Should Dr. Friedgood's request for parole be granted?

Yes:
- ✓ It is unlikely that if released, Dr. Friedgood would break any laws again.
- ✓ He should be released because of his advanced age and his good behavior in prison.
- ✓ He has cancer and his medical bills are very costly to the State.
- ✓ Sentencing should stress rehabilitation rather than punishment.

No:
- Dr. Friedgood's crime is inexcusable.
- The crime had "a negative impact on the victim's family."
- His release would undermine the seriousness of his crime.

Addendum:
In November 2007, the NY State Parole Board voted to grant Dr. Friedgood's release from prison.

Related issue:
Susan LeFevre was arrested in 1974, at the age of 19, after taking $600 from an undercover officer during a heroin drug bust. She walked away unnoticed from prison after serving one year of a 10-20 year sentence and moved to California where she married Alan Walsh, lived an exemplary life, and had two daughters and a son aged 15, 20, and 22 years old. Based on a tip, she was arrested in April 2008, more than 30 years after her escape. Should Ms. LeFevre be returned to jail?

Addendum:
After spending an additional year in jail, Ms. LeFevre was released in May 2009.

15

Q Should teenage lifers be given a second chance?

In August 1999, at the age of fourteen, Ashley Jones helped her boyfriend Geramie Hart, age sixteen, kill her grandfather and aunt. She also tried to kill her ten-year-old sister. Her grandmother was shot and stabbed, but recovered after being in a coma for a month. Both teens were sentenced to life imprisonment without parole. Despite the loss of her husband of fifty three years and her daughter, and despite suffering her own injuries, Ashley's grandmother believes that her granddaughter, now 23, deserves a second chance.

Should life imprisonment without parole be abolished for teenagers?

Yes:
- ✓ The United Nations voted 185 to 1 to support such a resolution.
- ✓ Teenagers are less mature and unaware of the gravity of their crime.
- ✓ Sentencing should stress rehabilitation rather than punishment.
- ✓ Teenagers, unlike other criminals, are more likely to change for the better.
- ✓ Teenage actions may represent a psychiatric impairment.
- ✓ Such sentencing represents cruel and unusual punishment.

No:
- • Some crimes are so terrible that life without parole is justifiable.
- • Such teenagers may do something similar in the future.
- • Teenagers should be responsible for their actions.
- • Some teenagers are beyond redemption.
- • Sentencing judgments are based upon individual circumstances.
- • Life sentences give comfort to victims' families.

Related issue:
In Roper v. Simmons, the U.S. Supreme Court banned the execution of those who committed crimes while under the age of eighteen.

Q

Should evidence obtained improperly be admissible in criminal court?

While driving from Vancouver to Toronto, Bradley Harrison's car was stopped by a police officer for no compelling reason, and 77 pounds of cocaine was found in the trunk. The exclusionary rule states that evidence obtained illegally is inadmissible in a criminal trial.

Should Mr. Harrison be found guilty of drug possession?

Yes:

- ✓ Selling cocaine is a serious crime which can injure many people and should not go unpunished.
- ✓ The exclusionary rule results in lawbreakers going unpunished.
- ✓ Police misconduct can be limited by internal discipline.
- ✓ The legal remedy for an unlawful search should be a civil suit.
- ✓ Most countries do not abide by the exclusionary rule.

No:

- Stopping the car was a violation of Mr. Harrison's rights and searching the car was unreasonable.
- Unreasonable searches are banned by the Fourth Amendment.
- Suppression of improperly obtained evidence will lessen police misconduct.
- How evidence is acquired is as important as what it proves.
- Perhaps the seriousness of the police misconduct should be taken into consideration when applying the exclusionary rule.

Addendum:
In Mapp v. Ohio, the U.S. Supreme Court ruled that improperly obtained evidence encourages disobedience to the Constitution and such evidence is not admissible in court. The Canadian court however, refused to exclude the evidence and Mr. Harrison was sentenced to five years in prison. (See pg.108)

Related Issue:
Bennie Herring was arrested for illegal amphetamine and gun possession based on a mistaken outstanding arrest warrant. Should an error made in good faith void the exclusionary rule?

Addendum:
The Supreme Court wrote that "The exclusionary rule serves to deter deliberate, reckless, or grossly negligent conduct [by law enforcement], and this case does not rise to that level."

Q

Should the three strike law mandating life in prison for petty theft be enforced?

California law requires a sentence of 25 years to life for a felony committed by someone already convicted of two prior felonies. This is known as the three strike law. The first two strikes must be serious or violent felonies, but the third strike can be any felony, which is defined as a crime punishable by more than a year in prison.

Gary Ewing who had prior felony convictions for burglary was found guilty of stealing three golf clubs from a golf shop and was sentenced to 25 years to life in prison with no possibility of parole before 25 years.

Leandro Andrade was sentenced to a 50 year to life term for stealing a handful of videotapes from Kmart.

Should these convicts have received long sentences for a relatively minor crime?

Yes:
- ✓ States should have the discretion to enact strong public safety laws to keep repeat offenders behind bars.
- ✓ The laws are intended to shut the revolving prison door for career criminals who are likely to be repeat offenders.
- ✓ The tough sentencing laws will send a message to career criminals and act as a deterrent to future criminal activity.
- ✓ Lenient judges will be prevented from dispensing lenient sentences.
- ✓ It is not unduly harsh to sentence thieves and petty criminals to life in prison.

No:
- • Harsh and disproportionate sentences violate the Eighth Amendment's protection from cruel and unusual punishment.
- • A 25-year prison term is usually imposed for someone convicted of first-degree murder, not shoplifting.
- • A person may not be imprisoned on the grounds of possible future crimes.
- • The law requiring convicts to serve their full sentences is swelling the prison population and increasing taxpayer costs.

> Addendum:
> The Supreme Court in Ewing v. California and in Lockyer v. Andrade upheld California's three-strikes sentencing law for repeat criminals.

Should there be a tamper proof national identification card?

A national identification card containing the carrier's photo and DNA has been proposed in order to improve national security and improve personal identification.

Should all residents be required to carry such a card and present it upon request by the proper authorities?

Yes:

- ✓ A tamper-proof national identification card would eliminate the problem of fraudulent work authorization documents and deter illegal immigration.
- ✓ National ID cards would improve national security.
- ✓ National ID cards would be effective in the fight against terrorism by preventing terrorists from operating under assumed identities.
- ✓ In the post 9/11 era, a trade-off of less privacy for more security appears to be reasonable.
- ✓ A national ID database system would speed up identity verification and reduce delays for airline travelers.

No:

- • National ID cards threaten our right to privacy. Government databases could easily be linked to other governmental and corporate databases and all of our movements, personal affairs, and transactions could be accessed by people who have no business knowing about our private affairs.
- • Promises of confidentiality could be easily breached.
- • The program would be very costly.
- • A national ID card increases police powers and could be abused and used to restrict our freedom.
- • The database could be used for government surveillance and to target government critics.
- • A mass-manufactured card can also be forged and a terrorist who successfully obtains such a card becomes a greater threat than if he had no ID at all.
- • The ID database computers and networks would become a target of hackers.
- • Ethnic classification on ID Cards, as in Nazi Germany and Rwanda, could lead to human rights abuses based upon group identity.

Q **Should private property be condemned under eminent domain for more lucrative private development?**

Under the concept of eminent domain, local governments may condemn private property for "public use" and provide "just compensation." Eminent domain has been used to seize private property to make way for roads or bridges and to improve blighted areas. The City of New London, CT is attempting to seize Susette Kelo's refurbished home, and evict 83-year-old Wilhelmina Dery from her home that has been in her family for more than 100 years in a non-blighted area of the Fort Trumbull neighborhood, for the purpose of upscale development which will include expensive apartments, marinas, retail shops, restaurants, and a conference center.

Should the government have the right under the "public use" requirement to team up with developers, condemn properties, and force people to sell their homes for the purpose of economic development that will increase tax revenues and improve the local economy?

Yes:
- ✓ Any public benefit from land taking is enough to satisfy the Constitution's "public use" requirement.
- ✓ The development will expand the city's tax base and result in higher tax revenues and increased economic growth.
- ✓ The new development would benefit the entire community.
- ✓ It allows revitalization of areas that otherwise would not get revitalized.
- ✓ An entire project should not be derailed because one or two owners will not go along with a voluntary sale.

 **Should private property be condemned under eminent domain for more lucrative private development?**

No:

- Seizing private property for development is an abuse of the power of eminent domain. Eminent domain should be limited to the forcible taking of people's property for roads, bridges, schools, and blighted property, but not for private development that will generate higher revenues for the city.
- If governments can seize private land and give it to new owners in order to generate more taxes, then all condemnations could be justified, and no home-owner or small business would be safe from large business interests.

Addendum:

The Connecticut Supreme Court ruled that the condemnations were constitutional in that a plan that promotes significant economic development is a valid "public use." In Kelo v. City of New London, the U.S. Supreme Court ruled that the government has the authority to take private property by eminent domain "pursuant to a carefully considered development plan, which was not adopted to benefit a particular class of identifiable individuals."

Q

Should the government have the right to practice racial profiling?

Racial profiling involves the use by law enforcement officials of race alone as a basis for criminal suspicion. Following Pearl Harbor, the Government justified racial discrimination against Japanese Americans in the name of national safety and security. In the late 1990's, the New Jersey State Police allegedly pulled over black male motorists, reasoning that they were more likely to be involved with crime. Hispanics have been targeted in the war against drugs. Following the September 11, 2001 World Trade Center terrorist attack, racial profiling has been employed against individuals of Middle Eastern descent in an attempt to prevent terrorists from boarding aircraft. In the war against Japan, in the war against crime, in the war against drugs, and in the war against terror, the interest of preserving national security has been put into conflict with the democratic ideal of racial equality.

In December 2001, an American citizen of Middle Eastern descent named Assem Bayaa, after clearing all airport security checks was kicked off a United Airlines flight from Los Angeles to NY while on his way to Saudi Arabia where he was employed as an auditor for Arthur Andersen & Co. He was told that he made the crew uncomfortable by being on board the plane.

Should Mr. Bayaa have been removed from the plane?

Yes:

✓ Racial profiling is a sensible police technique for managing scarce resources in the fight against crime.
✓ Civil liberties have to be compromised during wartime.
✓ Pilots are responsible for multimillion dollar planes with many lives on board and should be able to remove any passenger whom, for whatever reason, they consider a safety threat.
✓ Race should be employed as one factor amongst others in assessing suspicious criminal activity.
✓ El Al, the Israeli airline, is convinced that its extensive search procedures against young Arabs are an effective means of foiling attempted hijackings.

Should the government have the right to practice racial profiling?

No:

- The Fourth Amendment of the U.S. Constitution states that people have the right to be safe from unreasonable searches and seizures without probable cause. Being a member of a race is not probable cause.
- The Fourteenth Amendment of the United States Constitution guarantees all American citizens equal protection under the law.
- Hispanics are no more likely than whites to sell drugs, and Muslims are no more likely than whites to be terrorists.
- Focusing on one particular racial group may allow criminals from other racial groups to avoid capture.

Addendum:

The American Civil Liberties Union and United Airlines announced that they had reached a settlement in a lawsuit brought on behalf of Assem Bayaa and the American Arab Anti Discrimination Committee charging that the airline discriminated against Mr. Bayaa by removing him from the flight.

Related Issue:

Is affirmative action a justifiable form of racial or ethnic discrimination? In both instances certain individuals are given special treatment based on racial considerations. (See page 74)

Q   Should sodomy laws be overturned?

A sodomy law is a law which makes certain sexual acts, most commonly anal intercourse, a crime. Even though many of these laws target both heterosexual and homosexual acts, they are usually enforced only against homosexuals. In 1998 Texas police entered the apartment of John Geddes Lawrence and Tyron Garner and found them having anal sex. They were both arrested under a Texas law making same sex intercourse a crime, and each was fined $200 and ordered to spend a night in jail.

An Islamic court in Lagos, Nigeria issued an arrest warrant for Mallam Abdullahi Ibrahim who if caught could face stoning to death for having a gay relationship.

Should sodomy laws be decriminalized?

Yes:
- ✓ The constitution allows a "right to privacy" for freely-consenting adults.
- ✓ Sodomy laws undermine equality for gays in other areas, such as child custody and employment.
- ✓ Sodomy laws ban behavior that is extremely common amongst homosexuals and heterosexuals.
- ✓ Sodomy laws are based upon religious prohibitions on non-reproductive sexual activity, but not all heterosexual relationships are procreative.
- ✓ Homosexual relationships like heterosexual relationships are based upon love, passion, friendship and commitment and not only on the physical act of intercourse.

 **Should sodomy laws be overturned?**

No:

- Homosexual sodomy is regarded by a majority of people as immoral, unnatural, and unacceptable. It violates the purpose of human sexuality, which is designed to foster procreation.
- The government has an interest and right to legislate moral behavior and as Chief Justice Warren Burger noted, condemnation of sodomy "is firmly rooted in Judeo-Christian moral and ethical standards."
- As Justice Scalia wrote, "If sodomy laws are overturned, laws against bigamy, same-sex marriage, incest, adultery, prostitution, and bestiality are called into question."
- Overturning sodomy laws would result in there being no legal difference between heterosexual marriages and homosexual relationships.

Addendum:
On June 26, 2003, in the Lawrence v. Texas decision, the U.S. Supreme Court struck down a Texas state law banning private consensual sex between adults of the same sex on the basis of freely-consenting adults having a "right to privacy."

Q

Should same sex marriage be legalized?

Julie Goodridge and her lesbian partner of seventeen years, Hillary, who are raising an eight-year-old daughter, sued the Massachusetts Department of Public Health, claiming that banning same sex marriages violated the state's constitutional guarantees of equality and due process.

Should Ms. Goodridge and her partner have the same right to marry as a heterosexual couple?

Yes:
- ✓ Gays and lesbians are being discriminated against by not being able to marry legally.
- ✓ They are being denied governmental benefits, such as income tax savings, community property and inheritance rights, child custody awards, spousal citizenship, and insurance benefits which are only available to legally married couples.
- ✓ Marriage is a basic human right which should be available to everyone.
- ✓ Government should not regulate marriage and there should be a distinction between a civil marriage and a religious marriage.
- ✓ Gay marriages have as much value to society as heterosexual marriages.

No:
- • There is no right to marry whomever you wish. You can't get a license to marry your brother or sister, a young child, your dog, or more than one person.
- • Following legalization, there will be lawsuits against religious organizations that refuse to accept and allow same sex marriages, and objecting clergymen might lose their state license to perform marriages. Just as churches cannot exclude minorities they will be unable to exclude homosexuals.
- • Heterosexual marriage is the best means for healthy child development in a stable family.
- • The Bible outlaws homosexuality.

> Addendum:
> In November 2003 the Massachusetts Supreme Court legalized gay marriage.

Q Should prostitution be legalized?

In June 1993, Heidi Fleiss was arrested for running a call girl service catering to rich executives and movie stars. She received a sentence of three years imprisonment for pandering and tax evasion.

Should Ms. Fleiss' business have been legalized?

Yes:
- ✓ Legalization would require prostitutes to undergo regular medical examinations which would prevent the spread of sexually transmitted diseases.
- ✓ Laws against prostitution violate constitutional rights of privacy for freely consenting adults. What consenting adults do in private is their own business.
- ✓ Illegal prostitution encourages pimps and organized crime figures to buy and sell women on the black market and control women through the use of drugs and violence.
- ✓ Limited police resources should not be allocated for enforcing victimless crimes.
- ✓ Police enforcement has very little impact on prostitution. The prostitutes pay their fine and are soon back on the streets.

No:
- • Legalization of prostitution promotes and expands the sex industry and increases the demand for prostitution by men who now see the activity as being socially acceptable.
- • Legalization has been shown to promote illegal prostitution as many prostitutes try to avoid exploitation by sex businessmen, registration fees and medical examination fees, in order to provide cheaper sex.

Addendum:
In the city of Montreal, Quebec, there are clubs for "swingers" who wish to have consensual sex with one or more other people. The Canadian Supreme Court ruled against banning such clubs which promote group sex among consenting adults.

Q Should bigamy be allowed?

Bigamy is a marriage in which one of the parties is already legally married to another. Tom Green, a Utah Mormon, was convicted of bigamy for having five wives and was sentenced to prison. Green argued that he had a constitutional right to practice his religious beliefs.

Should Mr. Green's conviction be overturned?

Yes:

✓ The First Amendment to the constitution calls for a separation of church and state, and everyone should be free to practice his or her religion.

✓ Polygamy is permitted under Biblical law and many of the world's diverse cultures accept polygamy as a valid form of marriage.

✓ By overturning Texas' anti-sodomy laws, the United States. Supreme Court established a "right to privacy" for freely-consenting adults. Laws forbidding bigamy should be similarly unconstitutional.

✓ Government should have no role in regulating marriage.

✓ Polygamists believe in committed, consensual, and non abusive relationships.

✓ Polygamists like gays and lesbians would like to live their lives with those whom they love.

No:

• Bigamy oppresses and abuses women, and is unhealthy for children.

• The State has an interest in regulating marriage as an important social unit. The bigamy statute protects vulnerable individuals from exploitation and abuse, and prevents the misuse of government benefits associated with marital status.

• The law promotes mutual loyalty between husband and wife.

• Overturning the bigamy law would open the door to allowing pedophilia, incest, bestiality, and drug use in the privacy of one's own home.

Addendum:
In August 2007 Tom Green was released from prison after serving a six year sentence.

Q

Should the gay rights parade take place in the city center of Jerusalem?

World Pride, an organization of gays, lesbians, bisexuals, and trans-gendered people, in its effort to promote gay pride and dignity, planned to hold its 2006 international convention and parade in the holy city of Jerusalem.

Should gays be allowed to march in Jerusalem?

Yes:

   ✓ Everyone should have the right to demonstrate in a peaceful manner.
   ✓ Forbidding the march is a danger to democracy.
   ✓ The gay and heterosexual communities should be treated equally.
   ✓ The march should not be cancelled because of threats of violence.

No:

- The right to freedom of expression is subject to limitations, particularly when it offends the majority of the city's Christians, Muslims, and Jews.
- While everyone has the right to demonstrate, it is not always in their best interest to exercise that right.
- The gay lifestyle is a threat to the traditional model of the family.
- Jerusalem is a sacred city and an offensive and provocative parade could spark violence.
- The planned parade caused ultra orthodox Jewish men to riot in the streets, and the parade should be cancelled because of security concerns.

Related Issue:
Should the Neo-Nazi party be allowed to march in the predominantly Jewish holocaust survivor suburb of Skokie, Illinois?

Q Should laws prohibiting indecent and offensive forms of undress be adopted?

There is no federal law allowing or prohibiting public nudity, and so the legality of various forms of undress is left up to the individual states. In 1993 the Texas Court of Appeals upheld the conviction of Angie Carreras who was arrested for removing her shirt at an outdoor music festival, while her male companion, who also removed his shirt, was not arrested. In 1992, the New York Court of Appeals ruled that a group of women protesting while topless in a public park, did not violate a New York State nudity statute.

Should anti nudity laws be adopted?

Yes:
- ✓ Most Americans consider public nudity to be morally offensive. They do not want to see naked people walking down the street and do not want their children exposed to nudity.
- ✓ Anti-nudity statutes are not a limitation on personal expression which is protected by the Constitution, because nudity is an activity and not an expression.
- ✓ There is no evidence that public nudity results in fewer sex crimes, better adjusted individuals, or less pornography and violence, as supporters claim.
- ✓ Even if lewd intent is required to be arrested, it is difficult to distinguish between a lewd exhibition which arouses a prurient interest from non-lewd conduct.

No:
- Public recreational nudity is a popular activity which should be protected under the constitutional right of free expression.
- The law should be used to control nudity with lewd intent but should not be used to ban recreational nudity which has no sexual connotation and no intent to offend others.
- It is discriminatory to fine topless women but not topless men.
- Seeing someone completely nude is less sexually arousing than viewing sexually enticing forms of dress.
- Modesty is not instinctive but is culturally determined, and our notions of modesty are constantly changing.
- There is no evidence that exposure to non-lewd nudity promotes delinquency in minors, and children exposed to nudity are no more maladjusted than the general population.
- If people were accustomed to seeing a naked body they would not be shocked by such a sight.

30

Q

Should laws prohibiting indecent and offensive forms of undress be adopted?

Related Issues:

❖ Should breast feeding in public be treated as a crime?

❖ Should topless and nude beaches be allowed?

❖ Should a resident be allowed to mow her lawn while topless?

❖ Should one be allowed to bathe nude in a private backyard hot tub which is in the public view?

❖ Should adult entertainment establishments be allowed to continue featuring nude dancers?

Q Should a male to female transsexual be allowed to participate in women's sports?

Renee Richards, formerly Richard Raskind, had a sex change operation in 1976 and applied to play in the Women's Tennis Association U.S. Open. Mianne Bagger, who had a male to female sex-change operation in 1995, applied to play in the Women's British Open Golf Tournament.

Should transsexuals be allowed to compete in their re-assigned genders?

<u>Yes:</u>
- ✓ Transsexuals should be able to choose which gender they identify with, and how they feel about themselves, and then re-register their birth gender.
- ✓ Testosterone deprivation occurring after sex-change surgery, decreases muscle mass and decreases any competitive advantage.
- ✓ If trans-genders are prohibited from participating in sporting events because of a presumed genetic advantage, this raises the question of whether people born with genetic advantages for sports should similarly be prohibited from playing.

<u>No:</u>
- A person's gender should be determined by their birth certificate.
- Reassigned transsexual athletes might have an unfair advantage in some sports because androgens cause a greater muscle mass and an increased heart and lung capacity.
- Men who have undergone sex reassignment surgery generally have a competitive advantage over women due to their average greater height, muscle mass, and power, based on correspondingly different exposures to androgens. For this reason, in sports, men and women do not usually compete against each other.

Q **Should a male to female transsexual be allowed to participate in women's sports?**

Addendum:
The NY Supreme Court allowed Richards to compete as a woman in the 1977 U.S. Open.

Related Issues:
In 1979 Christie Littleton underwent male to female gender reassignment surgery. In 1989 she met and married Mark Littleton, an auto assembly line worker. In 1996, when Mark Littleton became ill and died, Christie Littleton sued her late husband's doctor for malpractice. In 1999, her suit was thrown out of District Court on the grounds that Christie was not his widow as she was really a man with male chromosomes and could not be legally married to Mark Littleton. The Court of Appeals upheld the trial court's decision.

Should someone who identifies himself or herself as a member of the other sex but does not undergo reassignment surgery be legally recognized as a member of their new gender?

Q Should libraries be required to filter internet access to sexually explicit material?

The Children's Internet Protection Act (CIPA) requires libraries to use internet filtering software to eliminate pornography and obscene materials which are harmful to minors, as a condition for receiving computer and internet related federal funds.

Should libraries be required to use filters?

Yes:
- ✓ The First Amendment guarantee of freedom of speech should not be used as a shield for the presentation of pornography to children.
- ✓ Because libraries are entitled to decide on which books and materials to make available to its patrons, it is similarly entitled to limit access to internet information.
- ✓ Filters are very effective in eliminating pornographic material.
- ✓ The law does not represent censorship of libraries, because they can decline to accept the federal funding, and the absence of filters would not be a criminal offense.
- ✓ Congress should be able to place conditions on public entities receiving federal funds.
- ✓ Librarians could unblock internet sites at the request of adult users.

No:
- • Filters restrict the First Amendment rights of Americans to view legal material on the internet.
- • None of the present filtering software can block objectionable websites without also blocking valuable constitutionally protected websites.
- • Because the method by which commercial filters choose which sites to block has been kept secret by its developers, the public has no knowledge of the basis upon which the blocking decisions are being made.
- • Supreme Court Justice Stevens said that although the government did not mandate filter blocking software, "an abridgment of speech by means of a threatened denial of benefits can be just as pernicious as an abridgment by means of a threatened penalty."

Addendum:
The Supreme Court upheld the Children's Internet Protection Act (CIPA) which requires the installation of filtering software on library computers which receive federal funding.

Q **Should paroled sex offenders be required to register with the police so that their whereabouts can be made known to the community?**

Megan's Law is named after Megan Kanka, age 7, who was raped and murdered in 1994 by a neighbor who was a twice-convicted sex offender. The law requires convicted sex offenders who are considered a risk to the community, to register with law enforcement authorities after their release from prison, so that if a sex offender moved in next door, you would be notified by law enforcement.

Should paroled sex offenders be required to register their whereabouts?

Yes:
- ✓ The law protects citizens and their children from sex offenders who are more likely than other groups of offenders to repeat their crimes.

No:
- Convicted killers are not required to register with authorities after their release from jail.
- Once convicted sex offenders serve their time in prison, they have paid their debt to society and publicizing their presence is an added penalty which punishes them for life.
- It encourages acts of vigilantism, and does not give paroled offenders the chance to merge back into society.
- Megan's Law deprives sex offenders of to their constitutional right to privacy.
- Constant societal pressure reduces the chance of rehabilitation for convicted sex offenders.

Should sex offenders be castrated?

Antonin Novak, age 43, who spent years in detention for sexual offenses, was found guilty of sexually abusing and murdering nine-year-old Jakub Simanek. He also admitted to abusing ten other boys. Advocates of castration believe that the murder would not have occurred had Mr. Novak been castrated after his initial offense.

Should sex offenders be castrated?

Yes:

- ✓ Castration (either chemical or physical) can eliminate the sexual urges of violent sex offenders.
- ✓ Laws preventing castration put potential victims at risk.
- ✓ The rate of repeat sex offenses after castration decreases from eighty percent to two percent.

No:

- Castration is irreversible. It is cruel and inhumane punishment and denies one the right to reproduce.
- The procedure is not always effective.
- The procedure should only be available on a voluntary basis even though consent is not always free and informed because sex offenders may opt for castration to avoid prison sentences.
- Castrated sex offenders might obtain and inject testosterone through illegal purchases.
- Rape is about power and not sexual desire.
- Castration of sex offenders may lead to castration of other groups such as mental defectives.

Should zoning laws be used to exclude adult entertainment?

Zoning laws are governmental laws requiring land to be used in a particular way. City officials in Renton, Washington, passed a zoning law prohibiting adult entertainment businesses from locating within 1,000 feet of any residential area, school, park, or church. Playtime Theatres, Inc. which purchased two theaters in Renton, Washington, with the intention of exhibiting adult films, claimed that the city zoning law violated their First Amendment constitutional right to free speech.

Can a city bar businesses through zoning?

Yes:

✓ The ordinance attempts to maintain quality of life, and is a valid governmental response to problems such as decreased property values and increased crime, created by adult theaters, adult bookstores, and nude dancing facilities.

✓ The ordinance is not concerned with the content of the films, but rather with the secondary effects of this type of theater on the community, and so the ordinance is a "content neutral" form of speech regulation with no limitation on freedom of expression.

✓ Adult theaters are not completely banned, and may open in other areas of the city.

No:

• Although some residents may be offended by the films, their viewing is protected under the constitutional amendment granting freedom of expression.

• In actuality, the ordinance was designed to suppress adult entertainment establishments, and discriminatory intent cannot be camouflaged behind zoning laws.

Addendum:
The Supreme Court held that the Renton ordinance in its attempt to preserve and protect the quality of urban life was a valid governmental response to regulate sexually oriented businesses.

37

Q   Should marijuana be legalized?

Marijuana diminishes inhibitions and produces euphoria. Those who smoke marijuana feel relaxed and sociable. Those under the influence of marijuana show a lack of coordination and impaired ability to perform skilled acts.

Should marijuana use be legalized for everyone?

Yes:
- ✓ The drug is entirely safe. It relieves stress and has medicinal value.
- ✓ The attempt to use the law to tell people what they may and may not consume at home is an invasion of personal privacy.
- ✓ The government could tax the sale of marijuana and use the income for other purposes.
- ✓ If we legalize marijuana, the black market would disappear as would the violence associated with the sale of marijuana.
- ✓ The law would ensure that people who use the drug for medicinal purposes, such as pain control, have legal access to it.

No:
- By legalizing marijuana, more people will use the drug.
- There is a tendency on the part of some users to progress to more dangerous drugs.
- Marijuana can be dangerous if smoked heavily. Its use has been associated with mental breakdown and once in a while it may produce hallucinations.
- A person driving under the influence of marijuana is a danger to himself and others.

Q Should marijuana be legalized for medical purposes?

Angel Raich, a California resident, is suing the federal government to allow her to use marijuana as a pain reliever, under her doctor's recommendation. She has found marijuana to be the only drug capable of controlling her pain despite treatment with multiple other medications. Federal law considers marijuana to be a dangerous illegal drug. California, however, is one of a handful of states which allows marijuana use for medical purposes.

Should Ms. Raich be allowed to use marijuana legally?

Yes:
- ✓ Sick and dying patients should be granted the right to use a medicine that has proven medical benefits.
- ✓ Federal law should not apply, because only interstate commerce regulation is allowed under the Constitution, and if the marijuana is grown and used only in California, then California law should apply.
- ✓ Federal power should be limited and states' rights protected.
- ✓ The legal sale of the drug would be limited to those who are using it for medicinal purposes, rather than for personal use.

No:
- • Marijuana is considered a controlled substance.
- • There is no fundamental right to an unproven medical treatment.
- • A pill called Marinol has the same active ingredient and is legally available.
- • Doctors may become intimidated to hand out prescriptions to those who want it rather than to those who need it.

Q

Should drug use be legalized?

Because of the detrimental effect of psychoactive substances, the U.S. Congress passed the Controlled Substances Act to limit and control access to drugs such as opium and cocaine that can make one "high".

Should all drug use be legalized and be made easily available?

Yes:

- ✓ Adults should be permitted to take whatever drugs they please, provided that they are prepared to assume the consequences of their actions and that they do not harm others.
- ✓ Prohibiting drugs increases their cost and increases criminal activity necessary to finance the habit.
- ✓ Because of the large profits to be made from illegal drugs, suppression is useless.
- ✓ Drug legalization would relieve prison overcrowding, unclog the criminal justice system, and free up police resources to fight other types of crimes.
- ✓ Many overdoses are due to fluctuations in the purity of street bought drugs. Legalization would standardize doses and avoid overdoses.
- ✓ Society already permits the use of some mind-altering substances known to be both addictive and harmful, such as alcohol and nicotine.
- ✓ Elimination of the huge profits to be made from illicit drugs would eliminate the inducement to police corruption and would eliminate drug dealers and organized crime figures from the market.
- ✓ Tax money spent on enforcing drug laws could be used for rehabilitation.
- ✓ Illegality in itself has attractions for young people.

 **Should drug use be legalized?**

<u>No:</u>

- Addiction to prohibited drugs affects not only the person who takes them, but his or her spouse, children, neighbors, and employers.
- Addiction threatens the safety of all other people; for example, commuters on a train or plane operated by someone impaired by drug use, or the 100,000 babies a year who are born addicted to cocaine.
- We don't have the right to do anything we want with our body. For example, we cannot walk down the street naked.
- Drugs themselves can cause violent behavior, and addicts given their drugs free of charge continue to commit crimes.
- The demand for drugs would rise dramatically were their price to fall and their availability to increase.
- If taking drugs is an individual's "choice," then all prescription drugs should be made easily available.
- If other dangerous drugs such as crack, PCP, and LSD are not made available, a black market will develop for their distribution.

Q Should clean needles be provided to drug addicts?

Clean needles are provided free of charge to drug addicts in the hope of slowing the spread of HIV infection and hepatitis caused by the sharing of contaminated needles. In 1986 Jon Parker was tried in Boston for distributing needles to drug addicts in violation of state law.

Should Mr. Parker be found guilty and sent to jail?

Yes
- ✓ Giving syringes and needles to addicts encourages drug use.
- ✓ Discarded syringes and dirty needles are still being dumped in public places.
- ✓ There is no definite evidence that exchange programs reduce HIV infection rates.
- ✓ Money might be better spent on educating teens about the dangers of illegal drug use.
- ✓ Needle exchange programs attract dealers who promote drug use.

No:
- • Clean needles help prevent the spread of HIV among addicts, their sexual partners, and the community.
- • There is no evidence that needle and syringe distribution encourages people to shoot more drugs or that it attracts newcomers to addiction.
- • Since drug addiction cannot be completely eliminated, it is important to minimize the damage that it causes.
- • Such programs provide an opportunity to teach addicts about the dangers of drug abuse.

Should tobacco products be regulated as a drug?

The Surgeon General has warned that cigarettes are a health hazard.

Should the Federal Drug Administration (FDA) regulate the sale of cigarettes?

Yes:
- ✓ Cigarettes are a dangerous and deadly product.
- ✓ Nicotine in cigarettes is an addictive drug.
- ✓ Smoking costs the nation billions of health care dollars each year.
- ✓ Cigarette smoking is a public health risk.
- ✓ Advertising and sale restrictions will save countless lives.
- ✓ Marketing to juveniles will be curtailed.
- ✓ More than 400,000 Americans die each year from smoking-related illnesses.

No:
- • The federal bureaucracy should not be expanded.
- • The FDA is already overextended and has limited resources to oversee drugs, let alone cigarettes.
- • People are aware that smoking is harmful and they still choose to smoke.
- • Cigarette advertising restrictions violate the cigarette companies' right to free commercial speech under the First Amendment to the Constitution.
- • Adults have the right to make their own decisions
- • The cigarette and tobacco industry is important to the economy.

Q

Should a drunk driver causing a death be charged with murder?

Martin Heidgen, 25, with three times the legal limit of alcohol in his blood, was arrested after driving at a high speed the wrong way on the parkway, ignoring drivers who had to swerve to avoid being struck, and finally crashing his pickup truck into a limousine, killing the driver and a seven-year-old passenger. Prosecutors claimed that he showed a depraved indifference to human life and should be convicted of murder.

Should Mr. Heidgen be convicted of murder and be subject to its harsher penalties?

Yes:

- ✓ A vehicle can be characterized as a weapon.
- ✓ He exhibited a total disregard for the lives of other travelers.
- ✓ His conviction will send a strong message that driving while intoxicated will not be tolerated.
- ✓ He should spend the rest of his life in jail because of the terrible crime that he committed and the lives he destroyed.

No:

- He was drunk and should not be compared to a cold blooded murderer.
- Intoxicated drivers are unaware of their actions.
- It is unusual to bring a murder charge in a fatal drunk driving crash, and a murder conviction would be unprecedented.
- One must have compassion for the family of the deceased as well as for the accused and the family of the accused.
- Alcoholism is a disease.

> Addendum:
> In an extremely rare decision, Heidgen was convicted of second degree murder for causing a fatal crash while driving intoxicated. He received a sentence of 18 years to life.

Related Issue
Should a driver who causes a fatal accident while text messaging or talking on a cell phone be charged with murder?

Q Should embryonic stem cell research be allowed?

Stem cells are undifferentiated elementary cells which have the potential to develop into all of the different types of adult human cells. Scientists believe that stem cells may grow into new tissues and replace aged, diseased, or injured cells. Embryonic stem cells are harvested at an early stage of development (usually three to five days after fertilization) from extra eggs stored in freezers at in-vitro fertility clinics. Public funding of embryonic stem cell research has been restricted in the United States.

Jane Jones was having difficulty conceiving because her Fallopian tubes were blocked secondary to previous disease. Approximately twenty of her ova were removed and fertilized with her husband's sperm. Four of her fertilized ova were implanted into her uterus with the hope that one would develop and continue on to a term pregnancy. The remaining ova were stored in liquid nitrogen to be used at a later date in case no pregnancy resulted. She and her husband became the proud parents of triplets. They decided not to have any more children and wished to donate the remaining ova to advance stem cell research.

Should these embryos be destroyed in order to extract and grow the contained stem cells?

Yes:
- ✓ Most Americans favor stem cell research and federal funding of such research.
- ✓ Progress has been delayed by the limited availability of cell lines.
- ✓ The most effective stem cells are found in embryos.
- ✓ Almost all stored spare embryos in fertility clinics will eventually die, due to operator error or equipment malfunction or will be routinely destroyed. They might as well have their stem cells extracted so that they can be of some use to humanity.

No:
- Although not as good a source of stem cells, stem cells can be extracted from alternative sources, for example, from umbilical cord blood or the outer amniotic lining of the umbilical cord.
- Embryonic stem cell research is opposed by those who feel that life begins at the moment of conception, and the extraction procedure which destroys the embryo is equivalent to murder.
- The fetus also has rights which should not be violated.
- The Bible is opposed to abortion.

Q

Should financial incentives be used as a means of securing organ donations?

In the United States, the buying and selling of organs is prohibited and organ procurement depends upon altruistic donation. Because of the shortage of donors, there is a significant risk of death to patients who are on a waiting list to receive a transplant. This shortage also leads to the problem of deciding which of the waiting patients should receive an available organ.

Should payments be made to increase organ donation?

Yes:

✓ Financial incentives would encourage organ donation, increase the supply of organs, and save the lives of those on the present waiting list who are unable to secure an organ.

✓ Everyone in the transplant business (doctors, nurses, pharmaceutical companies, hospitals) is paid and the transplant recipient receives a valuable organ. Why shouldn't the donor's estate be paid as well?

✓ In the United States there already exists a market for blood, semen, hair, and human eggs; why not for cadaver organs and non vital organs from living donors?

No:

• Payment for organs could result in brokering of organs for profit and exploiting people who need money, for example, by selling a kidney. It would give rich people the chance to get available organs first.

• Compensation for donating organs takes away the personal link and altruism in the act and decreases the emotional gain of the donor's family.

• Financial incentives could motivate families to decide against aggressive treatment and hasten withdrawal of treatment for financial gain.

• The human body will become a commodity that can be bought and sold.

Should financial incentives be used as a means of securing organ donations?

Should financial incentives be provided to surrogate mothers?

A surrogate mother is a woman who agrees to become pregnant and give over the child to a contracted party, usually an infertile couple. She may be the child's genetic mother, having been artificially inseminated, or she may be a gestational carrier, having been implanted with an embryo obtained by in vitro fertilization. In **altruistic surrogacy**, the surrogate receives no financial reward for her pregnancy, though all expenses related to the pregnancy are usually paid by the intended parents. In **commercial surrogacy**, sometimes called womb rental, the gestational carrier is paid to carry a child to maturity. It is illegal in some states and legal in other states. Some states have held that such contracts, while not illegal, are unenforceable. Commercial surrogacy is becoming an industry in India, where the ready availability of poor surrogates can result in substantial outsourcing savings.

Should financial incentives be provided for egg donation?

Egg donation is the process by which a woman provides ova for purposes of in vitro fertilization or for medical research. It has been dubbed egg trafficking when money is offered to women to have their eggs extracted.

Q

Should pre-implantation genetic testing be used to produce disabled babies?

Pre-implantation genetic diagnosis (PGD) is used to analyze the DNA of an early-stage embryo produced by in-vitro fertilization, for the presence of a variety of genetic conditions. One cell is extracted from the embryo in its eight-cell stage and analyzed. Embryos found to be free of conditions that would cause a serious disease can then be implanted in a woman's uterus and allowed to develop into a child. PGD allows couples at risk of passing on a serious genetic disease to have a child that is fully genetically related to them, who does not carry the genes of its parent's genetic disease. PGD has been most widely used to prevent the birth of children with chromosomal diseases such as Down's syndrome, Tay-Sachs, cystic fibrosis, sickle cell disease, Huntington's chorea, and Cooley's anemia. Some parents however, are intentionally choosing to implant embryos with malfunctioning genes that produce disabilities like deafness or dwarfism.

A lesbian couple, Candace A. McCullough and Sharon M. Duchesneau, both deaf since birth, chose to have a deaf child by intentionally soliciting a congenitally deaf sperm donor. Ms. Duchesneau was quoted as saying "A hearing baby would be a blessing. A deaf baby would be a special blessing." Baby Gauvin McCullough was born with only a slight amount of hearing in one ear. PGD could also have been used to achieve a similar result.

Should PGD be used to produce disabled babies?

Yes:
- ✓ Parents wish to have children similar to themselves.
- ✓ Some parents do not view certain genetic conditions such as deafness and dwarfism as disabilities, but as a way to strengthen family bonds.
- ✓ It is up to parents to decide what is best for their children.
- ✓ Life might be difficult for children who differ from their parents.
- ✓ Parents should be able to select genetic characteristics of their offspring as an extension of their right to procreate.

No:
- • Dwarfism and deafness are not the norm.
- • Most providers of PGD find such requests unacceptable.
- • The purpose of PGD is to avoid disease.
- • PGD technology could possibly be used to produce embryos on the basis of intelligence, beauty, athletic ability, and other non disease genetic traits.

Related Issues:
Should PGD be used to select a child's sex?
Should PGD be used to select a child who is a tissue match for an ill sibling suffering from a fatal disorder, and then use that child as a transplant donor?

48

Q Should post menopausal women receive donor eggs?

Studies have shown that fertility is related to the age of the egg and not the age of the uterus. Marilyn Nolen, a 55-year-old post menopausal woman, gave birth to a healthy set of twins after receiving eggs from a woman in her twenties. Similarly, Arceli Keh, after lying about her age, gave birth to a healthy baby at age 63 following test tube fertilization with donated eggs from a young woman.

Should Ms. Nolen and Ms. Keh have received donor eggs?

Yes:
- ✓ While age 63 might be too old to be having a baby, age 55 is fine because people are leading more active lives and living longer.
- ✓ More women are delaying childbirth until after their career is established.
- ✓ Older people may make better parents because they want their babies so badly, and because they are more emotionally and financially stable.
- ✓ Preventing egg donation to post menopausal women could be considered age discrimination.
- ✓ A woman should be able to do whatever she wants with her body.

No:
- Women do not ordinarily become pregnant after menopause, which occurs on the average at age 50, when their bodies stop releasing eggs.
- Elderly parents might not be in good enough health to handle the needs of teenagers.
- It is unethical to provide in vitro fertilization services to women who might not live to see their children grow up.
- It may not be fair to the child or to society, and the best interest of the child should override the interest of the woman.

Related Issues:
Should in-vitro fertilization (IVF) or artificial insemination services be provided to single mothers?

Should the number of implanted eggs be limited? (See page 3)

49

Q

Should non-violent mentally ill defendants be forcibly medicated in order to stand trial?

Dr. Charles Sell, a St. Louis dentist, was accused of Medicaid fraud, having allegedly submitted multiple false insurance claims. He was subsequently charged with trying to kill a former employee who planned to testify against him. Dr. Sell appeared psychotic at the time of his arrest and has been in a federal prison hospital for several years because of his psychotic behavior. His lawyers and government prosecutors agreed that he was unable to understand the trial proceedings or participate in his defense and was thus unfit to stand trial.

Should the court require Dr. Sell to take anti-psychotic drugs against his objections so that he could face charges of Medicaid fraud?

Yes:
- ✓ Forcing medication and restoring competence is the only way in which the court can determine Dr. Sell's guilt or innocence.
- ✓ Anti psychotic medications have few troubling side effects.
- ✓ Talk therapy is unlikely to be helpful.
- ✓ The anti-psychotic medication would allow Dr. Sell to communicate in a rational manner with his lawyer and allow him to participate in his trial.
- ✓ If medication cannot be forced, a defendant might take medication until halfway through a trial, and then abruptly refuse to continue taking medication and disrupt further criminal proceedings.
- ✓ Suffering psychotic patients should get medically appropriate care.

No:
- • Patients should have the right to refuse "mind altering" drugs.
- • The medication may produce harmful side effects.
- • "The government's interest in forcibly medicating an accused murderer may be essential, but its interest in forcibly medicating an accused thief is not."
- • The government should not have the right to drug its adversary.

Addendum:
The Supreme Court has long held that the government could forcibly medicate a criminal defendant who is mentally ill if that person posed a danger to himself or to others. However, forcibly medicating non dangerous criminal defendants and thus depriving them of their personal liberty and autonomy must be in the defendant's best medical interest and should significantly further "an important governmental interest."

Q Should psychiatric treatment be given to a condemned prisoner when restoration of competency will result in his execution?

Charles Singleton was convicted of murder and sentenced to death in Arkansas. In prison, his mental health deteriorated, and Singleton developed hallucinations and felt that demons were in his cell. In his hallucinations, he believed that he had already been executed. The prison began to involuntarily medicate Singleton with anti-psychotic medication after a review panel found that he posed a danger to himself and others. Singleton's psychotic symptoms eventually subsided, and an execution date was set. Singleton's lawyers argued that once the execution date was set, the forced medication became unconstitutional because it was no longer in his long-term medical interest. Rather than allowing Singleton to face the choice of being involuntarily medicated (and later executed) or left to suffer painful psychotic symptoms, his attorneys suggested that his execution should be stayed unless and until involuntary medication was no longer required to maintain his competence.

Should Mr. Singleton's forced medication be continued?

Yes:
- ✓ Society has a compelling interest in punishing offenders.
- ✓ Treatment will alleviate psychotic symptoms and restore competence.

No:
- The defendant has a liberty interest in refusing mind altering medication.
- Treatment will render him competent for execution and is therefore not in his best medical interest.
- The physician's role is shifted from being a healer to being an accomplice in the administration of the death penalty, and health professionals are prohibited from assisting in the execution of a condemned prisoner.

Addendum:
The U.S. Court of Appeals held, in Singleton v. Norris, that a mentally ill prisoner may be involuntarily medicated with anti-psychotic drugs to restore his competency for execution.

Related Issue:
Should Ahmad Edwards, a mentally ill criminal defendant, who was found to be technically competent to stand trial, be allowed to represent himself and act as his own lawyer?

51

Q

Should insurance companies pay for bone marrow transplantation surgery in breast cancer patients?

Bone marrow cells or stem cells from the blood are taken from patients with advanced breast cancer and re-infused after high doses of chemotherapy have been administered. Evidence from current studies on the efficacy of bone marrow transplantation or stem cell transplantation for the treatment of breast cancer is insufficient and inconclusive. Many insurers cover bone marrow transplantation for breast cancer, although some deny coverage for the treatment because it is considered experimental.

Nancy Levine is a 54-year-old breast cancer patient who has recurrent disease despite having had a mastectomy and conventional chemotherapy. Her physician recommended that a bone marrow transplant be performed.

Should Ms. Levine's insurance company be required to pay for such treatment?

Yes:
- ✓ Bone marrow transplants have been giving hope to patients with advanced breast cancer even though the effectiveness of the procedure has never been proven.
- ✓ Patients desperate for a cure are willing to do anything to try to live as long as they can without disease.
- ✓ The procedure provides breast cancer patients a potentially lifesaving treatment.
- ✓ Until conclusive studies are available, patients should not be impeded by limitations of health plan reimbursement and should be free to determine with the advice of their physicians what course of treatment is medically appropriate.

No:
- The treatment is still considered experimental and patients should be treated only as part of a clinical trial.
- The results suggest that bone marrow transplantation therapy is not necessarily an improvement over traditional chemotherapy.
- The treatment is very expensive (approximately $200,000). It may not be helpful, and has potentially harmful side effects.

Q Should patients with incurable disease be allowed to receive unproven experimental methods of treatment?

Joseph Hofbauer's parents insisted that their nine-year-old son with cancer receive Laetrile. Scientific tests have shown Laetrile to be of no benefit in treating cancer.

Should patients, especially those with a serious or life threatening illness, have the right to any drug or alternative medicine even though it has not been proven safe and effective and is not approved by the Food and Drug Administration?

Yes:
- ✓ Alternative therapies may provide for the patient and the family a sense that they are doing something to combat their disease as well as a sense of hope that they will improve.
- ✓ Even if ineffective, we should not disregard the potential power of a placebo.
- ✓ Patients with advanced cancer might not live long enough for the kind of drug testing which everyone agrees is very important in protecting the public. Seriously ill patients, with the advice of their doctors, should be entitled to any treatment that they choose.

No:
- Scientifically controlled clinical trials are necessary to ascertain how much good versus how much harm various treatment alternatives can be expected to achieve.
- The government must protect patients from possible harm by withholding experimental treatments and drugs until they are proven to be effective and safe.
- There may be significant risks involved with new unproven and untested treatments. Many new treatments sound promising but are eventually proven to be worthless and even harmful.
- Safeguards are necessary to prevent medical quackery and to protect desperate and dying patients who are willing to take great risks and turn to "slick salesmen" offering a false sense of hope.
- If there is some clinical evidence of a drug's effectiveness and safety, the FDA under its compassionate use program, will allow individual access to investigational drugs prior to completion of clinical trials.

Addendum:
The U.S. Supreme Court rejected the argument that drugs offered to terminally ill patients should be exempt from FDA regulation.

53

Q Should the Purple Heart be awarded for PTSD?

Post Traumatic Stress Disorder (PTSD) can be associated with anger, stress, nightmares, depression, inability to hold a job, and suicidal ideation. It has been reported that one in five servicemen may suffer from PTSD. The Purple Heart is a military award which has traditionally been granted to those soldiers who have been wounded in action and have suffered a battlefield physical injury.

Should the Purple Heart be awarded to servicemen with psychological injuries?

Yes:
- ✓ Granting the award will help remove the stigma associated with PTSD.
- ✓ Psychological injuries are as disabling as physical injuries.
- ✓ Soldiers with PTSD are granted disability payments – why not a medal?

No:
- • It is difficult to diagnose PTSD. Patients may fake symptoms in order to receive disability payments or to be relieved of combat duty.
- • PTSD might not result from any specific enemy action.
- • Historically, the award has not been granted for psychological conditions.
- • Granting the award might debase the honor of the medal.

Addendum:
The government in 2009 decided not to award the Purple Heart to soldiers suffering from PTSD.

Q Should mental health insurance coverage be on par with coverage for physical illnesses?

Health insurance plans usually apply more stringent coverage limitations to patients with mental rather than physical diseases. For example, mental health office visits might have lower reimbursements, greater co-payments and deductibles, and the number of treatments and the length of treatment may be limited as compared to physical health services. The Mental Health Parity Act would require health insurance companies to provide mental health parity, that is, to cover and treat mental illness the same as it does for physical illness.

Should mental health parity be enforced?

Yes:
- ✓ Mental illness is a disease as real as any physical illness.
- ✓ There are biological causes and effective treatments for mental illnesses.
- ✓ Early treatment will avoid complications and future hospitalizations.
- ✓ Private health insurance costs will decline as treated patients become more productive.

No:
- • Parity will raise the costs of private health insurance.
- • The mental health field has many vague maladies with many unproven treatments.
- • Talk therapy frequently has no end.
- • Drug addiction and alcoholism are behavior disorders and not diseases.

Addendum:
The Mental Health Parity Act was passed by Congress in 2008.

Related Issues:
Steven K, a forty four-year-old fireman with fourteen years of service, was found to be unfit for full fire duty because of drug and heroin abuse. Mr. K. claimed that his addiction is a disease entitling him to a disability pension.

Bob S. was dismissed from his job because of alcohol abuse. He claimed that his alcoholism was a result of workplace stress and he should be en-titled to a work related disability pension.

Addendum: In 1988 the Supreme Court ruled that "the consumption of alcohol is not regarded as wholly involuntary" and that the Veterans Administration could deny disability benefits to veterans disabled by alcoholism because their condition resulted from "willful misconduct." (See Traynor v. Turnage)

Q Should medical care be outsourced to other countries?

The Blue Ridge Paper Products Company, a self insured company in North Carolina, in an effort to save money, was prepared to send its employee, Carl Garrett, under a company sponsored plan, to New Delhi, India to have his gall bladder removed.

Should corporations be allowed to outsource patients for non emergency elective surgery and medical care?

Yes:

- ✓ By moving surgery overseas, American businesses would save money on hospital and doctors' medical fees, and allow corporations to become more competitive and more profitable. Medical costs in India are approximately 80% lower than in the U.S.
- ✓ Doctors in India and other countries are highly qualified.
- ✓ Outsourcing would be limited to patients who volunteer.
- ✓ Many uninsured Americans go oversees to obtain cheaper healthcare.
- ✓ Many oversees hospitals have new equipment and Western trained doctors.
- ✓ We are now living in a global economy.
- ✓ Patients could do some touring prior to their elective hospitalization.

No:

- The quality of medical care in India and other countries may not measure up to similar care provided in the U.S.
- Oversees hospitals and doctors are not licensed by U.S. regulatory boards.
- Medical liability payments may be minimal compared to huge payments awarded in the U.S. in case something goes wrong, and patients would have to fly back and forth while seeking redress in Indian courts.
- There will be job losses in the healthcare industry.
- Patients will receive treatment in an alien culture.
- Accompanying family members would have un-reimbursed travel and lodging expenses.
- Oversees care might become mandatory.

Should medical care be rationed?

In June 1987, the Oregon legislature decided to stop funding pancreas, liver, heart, and bone marrow transplants under its Medicaid program which provided health insurance to low income residents. The idea behind the Oregon reforms was that the legislature would decide each session how much money to allocate for Medicaid services, and a line would be drawn on a list according to how many services that allocation covered. Some six months later, a seven-year-old boy named Coby Howard, who was on public assistance developed acute lymphocytic leukemia and his doctors recommended a bone-marrow transplant. Oregon Medicaid refused to pay and Coby subsequently died of leukemia while his unemployed mother struggled to raise the money for a bone marrow transplant that might have saved his life.

Should the Medicaid program have paid for Coby's transplant?

Yes:
- ✓ All life is precious and should be preserved at all costs.
- ✓ It is unfair to withhold possible life saving treatments particularly to minors.

No:
- Rationing is necessary to curtail soaring medical expenditures.
- Oregon could not conceivably afford to pay for every medical care service for every person. By rationing care and not paying for costly services, such as transplants that would benefit relatively few Medicaid recipients, the State could expand insurance coverage to all state residents living below the poverty line.
- We cannot provide services that have any positive benefits to all patients, no matter how small and uncertain the benefits and no matter how high the costs.

Related Issues:
Should an uninsured, impoverished, undocumented, immigrant be entitled to free hospital emergency room care?

Should an uninsured, impoverished, undocumented, immigrant be given a scarce and expensive organ donation, or be maintained on permanent dialysis?

Q Should euthanasia be permitted?

Euthanasia (also called mercy killing) is the intentional termination of the life of one human being by another in order to permit the death of a hopelessly sick person in a relatively painless way.

There are different types of euthanasia:

- ❖ *Voluntary euthanasia: When requested by the patient.*
- ❖ *Non-voluntary: When no request or consent was given.*
- ❖ *Involuntary euthanasia: When an expressed wish to the contrary was given.*
- ❖ *Assisted suicide: When guidance or means are given for someone to take their own life.*
- ❖ *Active Euthanasia: Causing death by commission, such as giving a lethal injection.*
- ❖ *Passive Euthanasia: Causing death by withholding customary care or food and water.*

In 1983, twenty-five-year old Nancy Cruzan suffered a head injury with loss of consciousness following an auto accident. In the hospital a feeding tube was inserted with her family's consent, in order to maintain nutrition. She remained in a persistent vegetative state, and five years after the accident, when it became apparent that she had permanent and irreversible brain damage, her parents requested removal of the feeding tube and termination of her feedings under the assumption that a patient has the right to refuse treatment and that she would not wish to continue her nutrition given her present condition.

Should Ms. Cruzan's feeding tube be removed?
Should she be given a lethal injection had it been requested by her family? (Is killing someone worse than letting them die?)

Yes:

- ✓ Every adult who understands the consequences of his or her action, should have their wishes or advanced directives respected in decisions involving their own body and should have the right to refuse life-preserving medical treatment.
- ✓ Individual liberty is a fundamental constitutional guarantee, and everyone should have the freedom to be able to choose to die.
- ✓ Laws should not be used to restrict individual autonomy as long as expression of that autonomy is not harmful to others.
- ✓ Although people may disagree about what constitutes a good life or a good death, each person should be able to make his or her own choice.
- ✓ Prohibiting euthanasia encourages the practice of clandestine euthanasia.
- ✓ Quality of life is more important than the value of life itself.

Should euthanasia be permitted?

No:

- Most terminal patients seek suicide not because they are ill, but because they are depressed and depression is treatable.
- Adequate pain control can be achieved in almost all patients.
- Many patients consider suicide because they don't want to be a burden to their families.
- Suicidal intent is typically transient.
- With the increased cost of health care, patients with lingering illnesses may be branded an economic liability, and decisions to encourage death could be influenced by cost.
- Under the slippery slope concept, euthanasia, by diminishing respect for human life, has the potential to be misused by caregivers, and might spread from the voluntary to the involuntary, to include groups such as the mentally ill, the infirm and disabled, the demented, various ethnic groups, the poor, and the elderly, who are considered unproductive and a worthless burden to society.
- Human life is a sacred gift from God, which can only be taken by God.
- Life is the supreme good and is more important than the quality of life.
- Aiding a suicide is still considered a crime, and the police will intervene to prevent it.
- The ethical code of physicians is to save life and never to take life.
- There is always the possibility of a mistaken diagnosis, a new cure, or a spontaneous remission.

Addendum:

In December 1990, after witnesses presented clear and convincing evidence that Ms. Cruzan would have preferred withdrawal of life-sustaining treatment to continuing in a vegetative state, her feeding tube was removed (passive euthanasia) and she died two weeks later.

In 1998 Dr. Jack Kevorkian administered a lethal injection to 52-year-old Thomas Youk who was suffering from Amyotrophic Lateral Sclerosis (Lou Gehrig's Disease). Kevorkian was tried and convicted of second degree murder, (active euthanasia) and is now serving a 10 to 25 year prison sentence. (see the following page)

Q Should doctors be allowed to assist in suicide?

Physician-assisted suicide refers to a practice in which a physician upon the patient's request provides the means (usually a lethal dose of medication) or guidance for someone to end his or her own life. This differs from euthanasia because the patient rather than the physician will administer the lethal medication.

Dr. Jack Kevorkian, a retired pathologist, went on trial for assisting in the 1993 deaths of Merian Frederick, 72, of Ann Arbor, Michigan, who suffered from amyotrophic lateral sclerosis (Lou Gehrig's disease) and Dr. Ali Khalili, 61, of Oak Brook, Illinois, a bone cancer patient. Both died by inhaling poisonous carbon monoxide fumes provided by Dr. Kevorkian.

Should Dr. Kevorkian have been prosecuted?

Yes:
- ✓ Suffering patients should be given needed care and support, and not be encouraged to commit suicide.
- ✓ Life is sacred and physician assisted suicide runs directly counter to the traditional duty of the physician to preserve life.
- ✓ If physician assisted suicide were legal, there is potential for abuse. For instance, the poor or elderly might be encouraged to choose physician assisted suicide over more complex and expensive palliative care options.
- ✓ There is a difference between passively withholding treatment and actively killing a patient.
- ✓ Mistakes, such as inadequate treatment of pain, or errors in diagnosis and prognosis may have been made.

No:
- Physician assisted suicide may be a rational choice to escape unbearable suffering.
- The physician's duty to alleviate suffering, may at times justify the act of providing assistance with suicide.
- Just as competent people can hasten their death by refusing treatment, they (particularly the terminally ill) should be able to choose for them-selves the time and circumstances of their death.
- Banning physician assisted suicide is a limitation of a patient's personal autonomy and liberty.

Should doctors be allowed to assist in suicide?

Related Issues:

Should a book or internet site teaching methods of suicide be banned?

Should doctors administer medication and participate in state ordered executions?

Q Should caps be placed on medical malpractice awards?

Non-economic caps place limitations on the awards granted for pain, suffering and emotional distress. In 2003, the Texas legislature passed a law limiting compensation for intangible non-economic damage to $250,000 for victims of medical malpractice. There is no limit for economic losses, such as the cost of medical care or lost income.

Should medical malpractice awards for pain and suffering be capped?

Yes:

- ✓ Overly generous jury damage awards are the main reason for sky-rocketing medical malpractice premiums and rising healthcare costs.
- ✓ High malpractice insurance premiums have caused many physicians to stop practicing and threaten the availability of care in many communities.
- ✓ High awards for non-economic damages encourage more lawsuits and increases costs to fight frivolous lawsuits.
- ✓ Trial lawyers, who receive contingency fees of one third or more, are the main beneficiaries of malpractice suits.
- ✓ Fewer suits will reduce physician use of unnecessary tests known as defensive medicine.

No:

- Non-economic damages are a small percentage of total losses paid, and caps result in loss savings of only 1%.
- Insurers continue to increase premiums regardless of caps.
- Insurance regulation, rather than caps, is the solution to high premiums.
- Medical malpractice caps limit the rights of injured patients, and unfairly penalize stay-at-home parents, children and retirees with low incomes.
- Patients injured by medical mistakes are unable to recoup their full losses.
- One category of an injured party (the injured patient) is being singled out for special limitations in violation of equal protection and jury trial rights.
- Medical care has improved because of the threat of potential liability.

Related Issue:
Should punitive damages, which are meant to punish for fraudulent conduct rather than compensate for economic loss be allowed in civil suits?

Should a Boy Scout be dismissed for being an atheist?

Darrell Lambert, an Eagle Scout and a Boy Scout since age 9, who earned 37 merit badges, and donated multiple hours of community service, was ousted by the Boy Scouts of America, after he declared himself to be an atheist. Boy Scout policy requires a belief in a Supreme Being or higher power, though not necessarily religious, in order to maintain membership. Mr. Lambert said that it would be a lie for him to profess a belief that he did not feel, and if he did, he wouldn't be a good scout.

Should Mr. Lambert be dismissed because of his non-belief in a Supreme Being?

Yes:
- ✓ The Boy Scouts of America is a private organization which does not receive federal funding, and is therefore free to associate with and discriminate against anyone it chooses. The organization excludes girls, homosexuals, as well as atheists.
- ✓ Every church and synagogue and every club and private organization has the right to establish requirements for membership.
- ✓ If an applicant states that he is an avowed atheist, he does not meet the Boy Scouts' standards for membership and should not be admitted.
- ✓ The Boy Scouts attempts to instill values in young people and promote religious equality, but the Scout Oath, requires a Scout to pledge to "Do my duty, to God and my country." An atheist, in good conscience, could not agree to this requirement.

No:
- This country was founded on religious freedom, and Boy Scouts should have the freedom to believe or not believe in a Supreme Being.
- Discrimination has no place in scouting.

Addendum:
In 2000, the U.S. Supreme Court upheld the Boy Scouts' right to exclude gays. Forcing the Scouts to accept gays would violate the organization's rights of free expression and free association under the Constitution's First Amendment.

Q Should "one nation under God" be eliminated from the pledge of allegiance?

Michael A. Newdow, an atheist, whose young daughter is an elementary school student, brought suit against the Elk Grove Unified School District in California, claiming that his daughter's rights were violated by the daily teacher led recitation of the pledge of allegiance containing the words "under God."

Should the pledge of allegiance be revised to remove the phrase "under God"?

Yes:
- ✓ God has no place in a government which includes people with many religions and people with no religion at all.
- ✓ The pledge is an affirmation of a religious belief as well as a government endorsement of religion and violates the First Amendment to the Constitution which calls for a separation of church and state.
- ✓ A child's refusal to recite the pledge might be looked upon as a lack of patriotism.
- ✓ "Under God" supports monotheism as opposed to polytheism and atheism.

No:
- • The use of the term "under God" has little religious meaning, and is as Supreme Court Justice Souter said "so diluted, so far from a compulsory prayer that it should, in effect, be beneath the constitutional radar."
- • "One nation under God" is a patriotic and not a religious statement.
- • The statement does not endorse any religion.

Related Issues:
Should the term "In God we trust" be removed from our currency?

Should our Declaration of Independence which states that all individuals are "endowed by their Creator with certain un-alienable rights" be revised?

Should the South Carolina State Motor Vehicle Department continue to issue specialty auto-mobile license plates with the Christian cross and the phrase "I believe"?

64

Q Should Muslim women wear veils in Western countries?

British Prime Minister Tony Blair called the niqab, the full-face veil with a narrow slit for the eyes worn by some Muslim women, a "mark of separation." Jack Straw, the leader of the House of Commons, said that he did not believe that Muslim women in England should wear the veil.

Should Muslim women in England continue to wear the niqab?

Yes:

    ✓ Everyone should be able to dress and worship in any manner that they see fit, as long as their dress is not indecent and does not incite violence. If Muslims are not allowed to wear the veil, priests should not wear collars, nuns should not wear their habits, and Jews and Sikhs should abandon their head coverings.

    ✓ Cultural differences should be respected.

    ✓ Wearing a veil does not harm anyone.

    ✓ The wearing of the niqab is not the cause of tension; it is simply a sign of estrangement from British society.

No:

    • Western visitors to Arab countries are asked to wear clothing which blends in with local custom and religion, so as not to be offensive to local sensibilities. Muslims in Western countries should act in a similar fashion.

    • Immigrants should assimilate into their adopted country's culture or return home to their country of origin.

    • Security requires that people should be able to be identified by their facial features.

    • Wearing the veil is a form of masculine patriarchal oppression of women and has no place in the modern world.

    • Wearing the veil is an in-your-face political rather than religious statement.

Addendum:
Aishah Azmi, a 24-year-old teaching assistant, was suspended from her teaching duties in Yorkshire, England, after insisting on wearing a veil. The school district said that she could wear the veil outside the classroom, but that students found it difficult to understand her during English language lessons.

Related Issue:
Should Harvard University provide separate gym hours for Muslim women who do not want to be seen in gym clothing by members of the opposite sex?

Q

Should a Muslim woman be granted a driver's license if she refuses to be photographed without her veil?

Sultaana Freeman stated that a ruling requiring her to be photographed without her veil (a hijab) which covers all of her face except her eyes, in order to obtain a Florida driving license, infringed upon her Muslim beliefs and upon her right to observe her religion.

Should Ms. Freeman be granted a driver's license with a photo showing only her eyes?

Yes:
- ✓ In fourteen states, though not in Florida, a driver's license can be obtained without a photo.
- ✓ Driver licenses should not be turned into mandatory universal identification cards.
- ✓ Florida has issued several hundred thousand temporary licenses and driving permits without photographs.
- ✓ Courts in other states have ruled that individuals with sincere religious beliefs have a right to obtain licenses without photographs.
- ✓ Driving is a right and not a privilege granted by the State, as economic survival may depend upon one's ability to drive.

No:
- • Florida has a duty to protect the public and a driver license photo I.D. is the primary method of identification in the nation.
- • Absence of a photo I.D. could help terrorists conceal their identities.
- • In almost all Muslim countries (except Saudi Arabia where a woman is not allowed to drive) women do not cover their faces in I.D. pictures.
- • Driving is a privilege rather than a right.

Related Issue:
Lester Beachy, an Amish-Mennonite bishop, and others in his congregation rely on their cars for transportation, and take very seriously the second biblical commandment not to create any image of themselves. Their religion allows them to drive but not to sit for a driver's license photo as state law requires. Should Bishop Beachy be granted a license without a photo I.D.?

Q

Should a family be able to maintain malodorous farm animals in their backyard for religious purposes?

Stephen and Linda Voith and their three children live in the village of Angelica, New York, and are followers of the Krishna Consciousness Movement. Their religious beliefs include the reverence and protection of animals, particularly cows. A village ordinance states that farm animals cannot be kept on any village property of less than 10 acres unless a permit is obtained, which usually requires obtaining the permission of adjoining neighbors. Neighbors however are objecting to the family's four cows and a goat because of issues about public health and safety.

Should the Voiths be allowed to keep their animals on their three acres of property?

Yes:

- ✓ The Voiths are victims of religious persecution.
- ✓ Their freedoms are being violated because they keep animals for religious purposes.
- ✓ The Voiths say that their animals are holy and should be treated as family pets and not as farm animals.

No:

- The Voiths are violating a village ordinance and are keeping the animals illegally in the backyard of their home.
- Neighbors contend that the cows and goat are a threat to public health and safety.
- The neighbors consider the cows to be smelly farm animals that attract flies and soil public streets.
- The Voith's religious practices infringe upon their neighbors' rights.

Addendum:
The New York State Supreme Court ordered the couple to remove the animals from their property. This decision was unanimously affirmed by the Appellate Division.

Q

Should a manger scene be allowed on public property?

In Allegheny County v. ACLU, the American Civil Liberties Union argued that a Nativity Scene on the public property of the county courthouse be declared unconstitutional.

Should such a placement be allowed?

Yes:
- ✓ Over 90% of Americans celebrate Christmas.
- ✓ The display does not imply that the city is promoting one religion over another.
- ✓ The display was coordinated with the Chamber of Commerce to promote shopping during the holiday season.

No:
- The first amendment to the Constitution states that "Congress shall make no law respecting an Establishment of Religion." The establishment clause prevents the government from giving preference to one religion over another and such a scene therefore should not be erected on governmental property with public funds.
- By permitting a nativity scene, the government appears to be endorsing the Christian religion.
- Religious symbols, such as a cross, menorah, or the Ten Commandments can be freely displayed on private rather than on public property.

Addendum:
The U.S. Supreme Court ruled that religious symbols can be displayed on public property only if they make up part of a grouping of secular and religious symbols. The Court allowed a Ten Commandments display at the Texas Capitol and barred displays at two Kentucky Courtrooms, reasoning that the Kentucky display substantially promoted religion, while the Texas display served primarily a non religious purpose.

Related Issue:
Should the city of Pleasant Grove, Utah, be allowed to reject a request by Summum, a religious group founded in 1975, to display their Seven Aphorisms monument next to a Ten Commandments monument which had been donated to the park by a secular group in 1971?

Addendum: The. Supreme Court ruled that the placement of a monument in a public park is a form of government speech and it is therefore not subject to the Free Speech provision of the First Amendment. Summum's request was therefore denied.

Q   Should non celibate homosexual ordination be allowed?

In California, the ordination of Katie Morrison, an open lesbian Presbyterian candidate, was challenged, because the Constitution of the Presbyterian Church states that people who are ordained must practice fidelity if they are married or chastity if they are single.

Should Ms. Morrison's ordination be allowed?

Yes:

✓ Clergy should be judged by their ethical behavior and competence and not by their sexual orientation.

✓ The Biblical ban on homosexuality should be interpreted as referring to exploitative homosexual relationships and not monogamous, loving, committed relationships.

✓ Gay priests can better represent and guide the large number of gay congregants.

✓ Jesus never mentions homosexuality as being sinful.

✓ People are becoming more accepting of gay couples, and the Church should adapt to changes in modern society.

No:

• Judeo-Christian tradition holds that sexual relations are proper only between husband and wife, and that homosexual practice is sinful as stated in Leviticus 18:22 "You shall not lie with a male as with a woman; it is an abomination."

• Biblical principles no matter how unfashionable have to be maintained.

• Homosexual ordination would undermine Church teachings and put a stamp of approval on a sinful practice.

• Jesus overturned many Jewish Biblical traditions, but not the ban on homosexuality.

• Even if there is a gene predisposing to homosexuality, it doesn't mean that homosexual behavior should be embraced.

• Homosexuality can be overcome.

Q

Should clergymen adopt political stands?

Federal law states that in order for houses of worship to retain their tax-exempt status, they cannot endorse or oppose candidates running for public office and they cannot use their tax-exempt donations to further partisan campaigns. Clergy speaking in an official capacity cannot recommend a particular candidate or party, and should not indirectly imply whom they endorse or oppose. They are, however, free to advocate legislation and voice their opinion on controversial topics such as abortion, homosexuality, the death penalty, the sanctity of life, and euthanasia. Representative Walter B. Jones (R-NC) introduced a bill which would allow houses of worship to endorse, promote and contribute to candidates, and to supply staff to help with political campaigns.

Should politics in the pulpit be allowed?

Yes:
- ✓ Separation of church and state doesn't mean that the Church can't support or discourage one form of public policy over another.
- ✓ Religious beliefs should influence public policy, as religion is relevant to every area of our daily existence.
- ✓ The restriction is a violation of free speech which is guaranteed under the First Amendment of the Constitution.
- ✓ A clergyman should not be denied the freedom to promote religious doctrine that also happens to be a political issue.
- ✓ Peoples' religious beliefs and faith often influence the formation of their political beliefs, and the two are sometimes deeply intertwined. The act of clergy endorsing or opposing a candidate from the pulpit may arise naturally from their religious beliefs.
- ✓ Our values affect public policy. Religious organizations, as teachers of values, should be able to take political stands on issues.

No:
- • Being a clergyman does not provide special insight into politics.
- • Religious beliefs should not influence public policy. To do so is a violation of the principle of separation of church and state.
- • When a clergyman voices an opinion that justifies one view over the other, it mutes those congregants who feel differently. Religious leaders are more helpful as facilitators of discussions if they have not declared a definitive moral position themselves.
- • Polls indicate that most people think that churches and synagogues should abstain from supporting political issues and endorsing candidates, and that Houses of Worship should not come out in favor of one candidate over another during political elections.

Q Should religious groups be able to use banned drugs?

A Brazilian-based church with about 130 members in the United States wishes to import a sacred hallucinogenic tea drink called Hoasca for use in its religious rituals. Hoasca, however, is on the government's list of banned controlled substances.

Should the importation be allowed in this situation?

Yes:
- ✓ The government should not interfere with religious practices and should allow the free exercise of religion.
- ✓ The church should receive a religious exemption from the Controlled Substances Act. A religious exemption has been granted for peyote which is used by American Indians in their religious ceremonies.
- ✓ A powerful spiritual experience can be achieved by ingesting psychedelic plants.

No:
- The government has a compelling interest not to allow the free exercise of religion in this situation.
- The drug might be diverted to illicit use.
- The drug may have harmful medical effects.
- Importation may be a violation of an international treaty signed by the United States requiring nations to combat international traffic in illicit drugs.

Addendum:
In 2006, the U.S. Supreme Court ruled that the importation of Hoasca for religious purposes should be allowed.

Related Issue:
Should LSD (a hallucinogenic drug), from which some people claim to obtain a religious experience, be banned?

Q   Should blue laws be enforced?

Blue Laws, sometimes defined as Sunday closing laws, are laws designed to regulate recreational activities and commercial business on Sunday, the Christian Sabbath. These laws were first enacted in Colonial times to enforce moral standards, and required Sunday to be set aside as a day of rest and worship. Although most of these laws have been repealed or are not enforced, there are still many communities in the United States, especially those where religious fundamentalism is strong, that retain blue laws. Some of these laws have been retained as a matter of tradition or as a protest against the growing trend toward increasing hours of commercial activity in American society, or as a means of reducing traffic on Sunday and establishing relative peace and quiet one day of the week. Stores in Bergen County, NJ, one of the largest commercial shopping areas in the New York metropolitan area, are almost all completely closed on Sunday.

Should blue laws be enforced?

Yes:
- ✓ Blue Laws which promote Sunday as a day of rest and relaxation are secular in nature and do not violate the separation of church and state.
- ✓ These laws prevent making the Sabbath into just another day.
- ✓ Although Blue Laws may limit individual rights, they reflect the collective interests of the population.
- ✓ After Blue Laws are repealed, religious contributions decline, religious attendance drops, and drinking rates, and marijuana and cocaine use by youths go up.

No:
- Blue Laws violate the separation of church and state.
- They limit individuals' freedom of choice.
- Customers who find it difficult to shop during the week want stores to be open on Sunday.
- Sunday store hours increase tax revenues.
- Significant Jewish, Muslim, and Adventist minorities do not observe their Sabbath on Sunday.

Addendum:
The U.S. Supreme Court in McGowan v. Maryland (1961) ruled that Maryland's Blue Laws did not violate the Free Exercise Clause or the Establishment Clause of the First Amendment of the Constitution. While many of these laws are descended from religious traditions to encourage attendance at Christian churches, the contemporary Maryland laws had a secular purpose, namely to promote the health, safety, and welfare of the population.

Should one have the right to choose an abortion?

Prior to 1973, abortion was allowed only to save the life of the mother. In 1973, the U.S. Supreme Court ruled that during the first trimester, a woman and her doctor may freely decide to terminate a pregnancy.

Should abortions be made freely available?

Yes:
- ✓ Women should have freedom of choice.
- ✓ In the absence of legal abortions, dangerous back-room illegal abortions tend to proliferate.
- ✓ An abortion may prevent unwanted pregnancies.
- ✓ An abortion may be desirable because mothers may lack the financial resources to care for a child, and raising such a child at the present time might be difficult and disruptive.
- ✓ A woman may not want others to know that she became pregnant.
- ✓ Carrying to term might be detrimental to the mother's health.
- ✓ The fetus may have health or developmental problems.
- ✓ Conception may have occurred after rape or incest.

No:
- Life begins at the moment of conception.
- Abortion is equivalent to murder.
- The fetus also has rights which should not be violated.
- The Bible is opposed to abortion.

Related Issues:
Should a mother have the right to choose an abortion over her husband's objection?
Should minors be required to have parental consent prior to obtaining an abortion?
Should the morning after pill be sold over the counter?
Should tax dollars be provided to fund abortions?
Should sex selective abortions be allowed, particularly in countries like India or China where male children are preferred?
Should the Oklahoma law requiring that an ultrasound be performed and viewed by the prospective mother prior to an abortion be declared unconstitutional?
Should fertilized ova be used as a source for embryonic stem cells?

Q

Should affirmative action to increase minority enrollment in schools and in employment be continued?

Allan Bakke, a white applicant, was denied admission to the University of California Medical School despite the fact that his grades were better than most of the minority students admitted through the university's affirmative action program which used race as a factor in determining admissions.

Was the medical school correct in denying Mr. Baake admission?

<u>Yes:</u>
- ✓ Affirmative action allows minorities and women an opportunity for advancement and compensates for past exclusions.
- ✓ Affirmative action will narrow the nation's racial divide.
- ✓ It is in society's interest to support diversity in the classroom, and understanding between the races.
- ✓ Other groups beside minorities, such as children of alumni, veterans, athletes, and contributors to the university also get special consideration.

<u>No:</u>

- • Racial preference programs discriminate against white students and violate the equal protection clause of the Fourteenth Amendment.
- • University admission criteria should be based on merit and character and not on race.
- • Racial preferences should not be used as a means of eliminating racism.
- • The means (affirmative action) do not justify the ends (benefitting disadvantaged students).
- • The real problem is that public schools fail to prepare minority students for college.

<u>Addendum:</u>
In Grutter v. Bollinger and in Gratz v. Bollinger the U.S. Supreme Court ruled that colleges and universities can continue to consider race as a factor in deciding which students to accept for admission.

74

Should lesbians and gays be allowed to teach in public schools?

Should the California law (Assembly Bill 537) which prohibits discrimination on the basis of sexual orientation pertain to teachers?

Yes:
- ✓ Teachers should be judged by their competence and not their sexual orientation.
- ✓ Homosexual teachers can be mentors and role models for students who are questioning their sexual orientation.
- ✓ Students who are victims of anti-gay sentiments could be helped by gay teachers.
- ✓ The potential for child sexual abuse exists with both homosexual and heterosexual teachers.
- ✓ Allowing homosexual teachers in the classroom does not condone homosexuality.
- ✓ Everyone should have the right to express their sexual preference without fear of retribution.

No:
- Gay teachers will encourage impressionable children to become homosexual.
- Gay teachers will promote a homosexual lifestyle in the classroom.
- Gay teachers are more likely to be sexually involved with pupils than heterosexual teachers.
- Homosexual teachers openly propose behavior that undermines the moral values of the overwhelming majority of their students' homes.
- Gay teachers do not constitute proper role models for most students.

Related Issues:
Should same sex couples be allowed to attend a school prom?

Should students be allowed to wear clothing consistent with their gender identification?

Should student clubs that promote the homosexual lifestyle as normal and acceptable behavior, be allowed on campus?

Should homosexuals be allowed to become scoutmasters?

Q Should teachers adopt political stands?

The NYC Department of Education requires teachers to remain politically neutral and not endorse any particular candidate while in school. The teachers' union, the United Federation of Teachers, which supported Barack Obama, filed suit in Federal court in opposition to the ban.

Should politics in the school be allowed?

Yes:
- ✓ Teachers like all other citizens have a right to free expression.
- ✓ Teachers should serve as role models of political involvement.
- ✓ The adoption of political opinions should be encouraged in all schools.

No:
- Teachers have a special influence over their students who might then feel pressured to adopt their teacher's viewpoint.
- All sides of an issue should be presented without bias, so that students can decide for themselves which candidate they wish to support.
- Political favoritism should be prohibited because students are a vulnerable group and they might feel intimidated if they support a different candidate than their teacher.

> Addendum:
> A federal judge upheld New York City's policy requiring political neutrality in the classroom. Teachers will not be able to wear political pins, hang political posters, or support a particular candidate while at work in school.
>
> The Virginia Education Association was criticized for encouraging their students to vote Democratic.

Should government scholarships be awarded to religion majors?

The Promise Scholarship program in the State of Washington grants college scholarship money to needy high school students. Joshua Davey was advised that his plan to major in theology at Northwest College in Kirkland, Washington, made him ineligible for a state-funded scholarship.

Should Mr. Davey be granted scholarship aid to prepare for the ministry?

Yes:
- ✓ Failure to grant aid is a form of religious discrimination.
- ✓ The Washington Constitution's restriction on funding discriminates against religion and violates the First Amendment of the Constitution which allows the free exercise of religion.

No:
- Failure to fund religious activity is not the same as religious discrimination, since scholarships may be granted for students who take religion courses at religious colleges, as long as they do not major in theology.
- Taxpayers should not be forced to pay for religious schooling.
- The state constitution prohibits funding any religious "worship, exercise or instruction."
- As Chief Justice Renquist wrote, "Training someone to lead a congregation is an essentially religious endeavor."

Addendum:

The First Amendment provides that "Congress shall make no law respecting an establishment of religion [the establishment clause], or prohibiting the free exercise thereof [the free exercise clause]." The establishment clause prohibits governmental established religion. The free exercise clause prohibits governmental interference with religion. These two clauses are frequently in tension with each other. Davey contended that excluding theology majors from receiving scholarships, targeted religion and limited its free exercise, and was therefore, presumed to be unconstitutional. Which part of the Constitution should apply in the Davey case?

In Locke v. Davey (February 2004), the Supreme Court of the United States upheld the state of Washington's right to deny a tax-funded scholarship to a college student studying to be a minister and that such denial does not violate the free exercise rights of individuals.

Q Should non-denominational prayers be allowed in public schools?

The NY State Board of Regents authorized the recitation every morning in the public schools of the following non-denominational prayer. "Almighty God, we acknowledge our dependence upon Thee, and we beg Thy blessings upon us, our parents, our teachers and our country."

Should such a prayer recitation be allowed?

Yes:
- ✓ The prayer is so generally worded so as not to offend anyone's religious beliefs.
- ✓ No student is compelled to recite the prayer. They could be excused from the classroom or stay in class and remain silent.
- ✓ Each day's session of the Supreme Court starts with the invocation: "God save the United States and this Honorable Court." "In God we Trust" is on our coinage. The Pledge of Allegiance contains the words "one Nation under God, indivisible, with liberty and justice for all." The Declaration of Independence includes the phrase: "with a firm reliance on the protection of Divine Providence."
- ✓ School prayer increases our culture's moral and ethical values.
- ✓ Allowing voluntary prayer does not establish an unconstitutional "official religion."

No:
- • State-sponsored prayer marginalizes religious minorities.
- • Atheists who deny the existence of God, and agnostics who are uncertain about the existence of God are opposed to any mention in prayer of God or a Supreme Being.
- • Many liberals, even those who are religious, believe in the complete separation of church and state, and oppose school prayer on principle.
- • An invocation of God's blessings is a religious activity which cannot be forced upon students.

Should non-denominational prayers be allowed in public schools?

Addendum:

School parents sued in New York State Court, claiming that the prayer requirement ran counter to the First Amendment of the U.S. Constitution which requires that "Congress shall make no law respecting an establishment of religion." The Court rejected their suit, saying that the prayer was constitutional, as long as the school did not compel any student to recite the prayer over their parents' objection. The New York Court of Appeals upheld this ruling and the parents then appealed to the U.S. Supreme Court which on June 25, 1962, ruled 7 to 1 that it was unconstitutional for a government agency like a school to require students to recite prayers even if they are voluntary and denominationally neutral.

The first case to come to the Supreme Court regarding school prayer was that of Engel v. Vitale in 1961. In this decision, the Court declared unconstitutional the inclusion of state-sponsored school prayer as a part of instruction in public schools.

Q Should formal prayers be invoked prior to school football games?

Galveston's Santa Fe Independent School District permitted "student-selected, student-given, non-sectarian, non-proselytizing" prayers to be read over the PA system at football games.

Should such prayers be allowed?

Yes:
- ✓ The purpose of such prayers as stated by the school board was "to solemnize the event, to promote good sportsmanship and student safety, and to establish the appropriate environment for the competition."
- ✓ Public prayer lends an air of significance to sporting events.

No:
- The state may not endorse a religious message, even if the majority of the people want it.
- Prayer, if truly initiated by an individual student, is protected free speech, but state-sponsored public prayer or religious activity is unconstitutional.
- Formal prayer coerces attendees into participating in a religious activity.
- Prayer sponsorship sends a message to members of the audience who are non-adherents that they are outsiders.
- The Constitution forbids not only state practices that endorse a particular religion, but also those practices that endorse religion over non-religion.

Should formal prayers be invoked prior to school football games?

Addendum:
The Supreme Court declared that public schools cannot allow students to conduct formal prayers before school games. The Court rejected the arguments by the school district that the prayer was not compulsory or coercive because nobody was required to attend the game or to participate in the invocation. The ruling stated: "The Constitution demands that schools not force on students the difficult choice between whether to attend these games or risk facing a personally offensive religious ritual. Even if we regard every high school student's decision to attend a home football game as purely voluntary, we are nevertheless persuaded that the delivery of a pre-game prayer has the improper effect of coercing those present to participate in an act of religious worship."

Related Issue:
Is a moment of silence constitutional?

Addendum:
In Wallace v. Jaffe (1985), the U.S. Supreme Court ruled that an Alabama "moment of silence" law which allowed public schools in the state to start each classroom day with a moment "for meditation or voluntary prayer" was unconstitutional. The court decided that the sole purpose in passing the law was to promote religion.

Q

Should religious attire such as head scarves, skullcaps, turbans, and large crosses be banned in public schools?

Under a new French law which bans religious symbols in public schools, two Muslim girls were suspended from school for wearing head scarves. Similarly, Sikh boys will not be able to wear turbans nor Jewish boys to wear skullcaps.

Should the girls' suspension remain in force?

Yes:

- ✓ The law is necessary to help protect France's secular culture.
- ✓ The law will enforce the strict division between church and state.
- ✓ Eliminating religious symbols in schools will help immigrants integrate into society.
- ✓ Some feminists believe that the veil is a symbol of oppression which is used by men to dominate women.
- ✓ Head scarves are being used more as a political statement than as a religious symbol.

No:

- Everyone should be able to practice his or her religion and beliefs peacefully without governmental control, as long as they do not disrupt school or interfere with the rights of others.
- Banning the head coverings will not protect secular culture, but will make people more defiant and determined to wear them, and will encourage Islamic radicalism.
- State coercion in matters of religion does not bring religious peace, but rather leads to conflict and division.
- Banning head coverings will more likely lead to a fragmented rather than an integrated society.

Related Issues:

Faiza Silmi, 32, was denied French citizenship because she chose to wear an Islamic facial veil called a niqab. The court held that her radical Islamic practice was incompatible with the French value of sexual equality.

Turkey has banned the wearing of head scarves in public universities, stating that it violates the constitutional principle of secularism.

Q Should students be required to wear uniforms?

Benjamin Kirk, whose minor son is an elementary school student, brought suit against the Natalia Independent School District which required its students to wear school uniforms.

Should Mr. Kirk's son be required to wear a school uniform?

Yes:
- ✓ Uniforms promote equality amongst students.
- ✓ Students do not have to think about what to wear and kids whose parents could not afford to buy the latest fad would not be embarrassed.
- ✓ Uniforms promote school pride.
- ✓ School uniforms increase school safety by preventing outsider infiltration.
- ✓ Uniforms are less costly than stylish clothing.
- ✓ Many jobs require uniforms.

No:

- Uniforms stifle diversity and individuality and learning to live with diversity is an important part of education and maturity.
- A student should be allowed to wear, for example, an anti war T-shirt if he so desires.
- One's type of dress is a form of symbolic expression and should be protected under the First Amendment of the Constitution which protects freedom of speech.
- While uniforms may be less costly, students will still need other clothing for non school activities.
- Parents should decide how their children dress.

 **Q** **Should parents be allowed to opt out of State mandated vaccination programs for their children?**

Dan McCarthy's eleven-year-old daughter was suspended from school for failing to receive immunizations as required under Arkansas law. Mr. McCarthy argued that mandatory vaccinations were unconstitutional and violated his rights under the First and Fourteenth Amendments which allow the free exercise of religion.

Should parents decide which, if any, vaccinations their children should receive?

Yes
- ✓ Informed consent is an ethical principle in the practice of modern medicine and implies the right to refuse consent for vaccinations or other medical treatments. Individual patients in consultation with their physicians should determine what is best for them and for their families.
- ✓ Government officials should not have the power to compel medical care.
- ✓ Vaccinations may be an infringement of personal religious beliefs.

No:
- • Vaccinations serve important public health purposes and have been very effective in reducing or eliminating communicable diseases.
- • The presence of non immunized schoolchildren can lead to disease among children who have received their shots because vaccinations do not work 100% of the time.
- • All states already offer medical exemptions for those individuals who are immunocompromised or have allergic reactions to vaccine constituents. Religious exemptions are allowed in 48 states (West Virginia and Mississippi do not). No additional exemptions should be offered.
- • Individual rights must be weighed against the public good and the state's interest in protecting society against the spread of disease. Individual freedoms must be enjoyed in ways that do not interfere with or create risks for others.

Addendum:
In Henning Jacobson v. Massachusetts, the U.S. Supreme Court upheld the right of states to compel compulsory vaccination.

Related Issue:
Should drug companies be free from liability for vaccine injuries?

Q

Should students be given monetary incentives if they excel on state achievement tests?

The New York City Board of Education, the largest public school system in the United States, as well as other national and international school boards, is experimenting with providing financial incentives to improve school attendance and improve performance on standardized achievement tests.

Should the student reward program (pay for performance) continue?

Yes:

✓ Incentives motivate kids particularly among poor and minority students.
✓ Studies have found financial incentives to be effective.
✓ Students take their studies and tests much more seriously.
✓ Rich kids are frequently rewarded by their parents for high test scores.
✓ In our capitalist society, people are motivated by money.
✓ Cash awards for doing well makes achievement more socially acceptable.

No:

• Cash incentives can diminish the desire to learn for non-financial reasons.
• It is uncertain whether incentives work. Studies have had mixed results.
• The correlation between education and future income ought to be sufficient motivation.
• Incentives will lead kids to demand money for, say, taking out the garbage.
• We need to value education and learning for the sake of learning.
• Rather than money, we need better qualified and motivated teachers.
• Bribery in any form is not desirable.

Related Issue:
It has been stated that teacher effectiveness is the most important factor in promoting learning. Rather than rewarding students, should teachers be rewarded by linking their pay to student achievement?

Q. Should parents be granted school vouchers for their children to attend any school of their choice?

The City of Cleveland established a program to provide vouchers worth up to $2,250 for low income students for use in any school of their choosing, whether public or private, and without regard to the school's religious affiliation.

Should such a program be approved?

Yes:

✓ Funding of public education depends mostly on local property taxes, so that schools in richer neighborhoods are better funded than inner city poor neighborhood schools. Many minority students will now be able to escape from poor inner city schools.

✓ Inner city schools will have to improve in order to stay competitive.

No:

• Schooling is a governmental obligation, and in the United States there is a long tradition of tax supported public, but not private education.

• The First Amendment to the Constitution which states that "Congress shall make no law respecting an Establishment of Religion" prevents public tuition aid to religious schools.

• Vouchers will "skim away" the better students, and educational quality in inner city schools will deteriorate even further.

• Only slight differences in achievement have been found between those students in inner city schools and those who have transferred to private schools under a voucher program.

Q Should teachers be allowed to carry concealed weapons into the classroom?

A school board in rural northern Texas, unlike any other school board in the country, is allowing teachers to carry concealed weapons into the classroom.

Should teachers carry guns to protect their students?

Yes:

✓ The School Board has a duty to protect its students.

✓ The county sheriff's office is 17 miles away and will be delayed during an emergency.

✓ There has been a recent surge in school shootings. Twelve students and one teacher were murdered in Columbine High School near Denver in 1999. Thirty two people were killed at Virginia Tech in 2007.

✓ It is too expensive to hire multiple armed peace officers.

✓ Teachers will receive training prior to being authorized to carry a concealed weapon.

✓ Israel and Thailand have well-trained teachers carrying weapons in an effort to protect their students.

No:

• Teachers are trained to teach - not to police.

• The teacher's weapon might discharge by accident and cause harm.

• A teacher-student argument could lead to a fatality.

Q Should a Hebrew language charter school be approved?

Charter schools are autonomous, privately run, elementary or secondary schools, financed by public funds that cater to a particular language or culture, while also teaching all state required courses.

The Ben Gamla Charter School, which recently opened in Florida, concentrates on teaching Hebrew language and culture. Students spend one period a day learning Hebrew language and culture, and have a second daily class, such as science, conducted in Hebrew.

Should a charter be granted to the Ben Gamla School?

Yes:
- ✓ Hebrew is a language, not a religion, and such a school does not violate the principle of separation of church and state.
- ✓ Citizens should be proficient in other languages, and the school is no different from other schools with dual language programs.
- ✓ Latin and Hebrew have always been taught in public schools with no association with the Catholic or Jewish religion.
- ✓ There is no religious instruction and prayers are not recited.
- ✓ Students don't have to be Jewish to attend the school.
- ✓ Hebrew will be taught in a cultural rather than in a religious context.
- ✓ Hebrew texts will be studied as literature and not as religious instruction.

No:
- Once a Jewish charter school is established, other religious groups will want to open similar schools according to their religious tradition.
- Jewish culture cannot be distinguished from Judaism and cannot be taught outside of a religious context. For example, the school will serve kosher meals and have a rabbi as its principal.
- The cost of cultural education should be borne by those who desire such a curriculum.
- Public supported dedicated foreign language schools promote a separation and isolation of people.

Related Issue:
Should a charter be granted to the Khalil Gibran International Academy in Brooklyn, NY, which will focus on Arabic language and Muslim culture?

Q Should online virtual public schools be allowed?

In Milwaukee, Tracie Weldie's three elementary school children, instead of attending a regular school, are taught by their mother with the help of lessons prepared by a publicly financed virtual internet school.

Should home schooling via the internet be allowed?

Yes:
- ✓ Online schooling improves the efficiency of education.
- ✓ Home schooling via the internet alleviates school overcrowding.
- ✓ Students can learn at any time or place and at their own pace. There is no wasted travel time.
- ✓ Students in remote areas can be exposed to a variety of courses and a wide range of curricula not locally available.
- ✓ Online teachers are able to monitor student progress.
- ✓ The schools meet state and federal regulatory requirements.
- ✓ It may be appropriate for students confined to home for health reasons.

No:
- • Children need social interaction with other students and teachers, and isolated online education is therefore inappropriate.
- • An online school is home schooling at public expense, and parents should not be able to teach their children at public expense.
- • Funds for education are being diverted from regular brick and mortar schools.
- • Students are missing out on classroom discussion and divergent opinions.
- • Science labs require hands on experience and are not available online.
- • Extracurricular activities such as clubs and team sports are not available online.
- • Online learning should only be allowed to supplement traditional schooling rather than providing children with all of their education.

Q

Should a public university recognize and support a fraternity which is open only to Christians?

The University of North Carolina at Chapel Hill stated that "membership in recognized student groups must be open to all students on a nondiscriminatory basis." It therefore did not extend official recognition to Alpha Iota Omega, a religious fraternity which had within its by-laws clauses that required a particular religious affiliation for membership, and limited its membership to Christian men. The fraternity was not banned from the campus, but was declared to be ineligible for university funding and access to university facilities for meetings.

Should the fraternity be required to open its doors to all comers?

Yes:
- ✓ All students should be allowed membership in any recognized student group.
- ✓ The Fourteenth Amendment to the Constitution provides for freedom from discrimination and the North Carolina Constitution also states: "No person shall be denied the equal protection of laws; nor shall any person be subjected to discrimination by the State because of race, color, religion, or national origin."
- ✓ While a private group might associate along religious or racial lines, the university is a public institution, and therefore cannot discriminate.

No:
- • The First Amendment provides for freedom of association.
- • Compliance would require the Black Student Movement to be open to white students. Women's advocacy groups would have to accept men and Jewish student groups would have to accept members of other faiths who might eventually take control over the organization.

Related Issue:
Should the private Phoenix Country Club be allowed to continue to forbid entrance of its female members to the men's grill room, or should it be considered equivalent to a public accommodation subject to anti-discrimination laws, because it receives income from non members who rent the facility for banquets, speeches, and meetings?

Q Should public schools provide sex education, birth control information, and condoms to students?

The Holyoke School decided to make condoms available to students in grades 6-12 after the students received parental consent and counseling.

Should public schools be funded for this type of education?

Yes:

- ✓ Counseling and school condom availability will reduce unintended pregnancy in teenagers, as well as decrease the risk of acquiring AIDS and other sexually transmitted diseases.
- ✓ Condom availability is not associated with greater sexual activity.
- ✓ Information on contraceptives, birth control, abortion, masturbation, as well as information on heterosexual and homosexual relationships and other methods of preventing pregnancy, are appropriate topics for sex education programs.

No:

- Providing condoms and information about birth control in school encourages young people to have sexual intercourse.
- Sex education programs appear to endorse early adolescent sex.
- Students should be taught abstinence and they should delay sexual experience until marriage.
- Talking about abstinence and condoms at the same time, conveys a mixed and confusing message to young people.
- Sex education is best left to parents.
- Sex education is okay, but schools shouldn't distribute condoms.

Related Issue:
Should homosexuality and bisexuality be taught in a sex education course as an alternative or as a degenerative lifestyle?

91

Q — Should a government-funded museum sponsor offensive art?

The Brooklyn Museum of Art sponsored an art exhibit featuring Chris Ofili's painting of the Virgin Mary surrounded by elephant dung and sexually explicit photos. New York City's Mayor, Rudolph Guiliani, called the painting offensive and anti-Catholic, and tried to have the museum remove the painting from the exhibit by threatening to suspend the museum's lease and its city funding.

Should the museum be forced to remove the painting from its exhibit?

Yes:
- ✓ The picture is insulting to the Virgin Mary and to Catholics.
- ✓ The painting denigrates religion.
- ✓ The museum violated its contractual obligation to display appropriate shows for the citizens of New York.
- ✓ This type of painting can be exhibited in a private gallery, but because of its offensive nature, it should not be supported with taxpayer funds.

No:
- • Forcing removal of the painting is a form of censorship and is contrary to the constitutional right of freedom of expression.
- • There should be a separation of art and state.
- • The artwork is thought provoking, and the exhibition serves as a medium for expressing new ideas.
- • Censorship limits the role that art plays in society.
- • Tastefulness in art is subjective and should not be determined by politicians.
- • No one is forced to visit the exhibit.

> Addendum:
> Federal Judge Nina Gershon ruled that Guiliani's withdrawal of funding violated the First Amendment.

Related Issues:
The publication by a Danish newspaper of a cartoon denigrating the Muslim Prophet Muhammed resulted in anger across the Muslim world with calls for an anti-Danish boycott and anti-Western protests and riots.

In France, Muslims protested the performance of a 1741 play by Voltaire, which mocked religion and described Muhammed as a tyrant and a fanatic. Voltaire has been quoted to have said "I disapprove of what you say, but I will defend to the death your right to say it."

Q   Should jury deliberations be televised?

Texas prosecutors were seeking the death penalty against Cedric Harrison who was charged with the murder of Felix Sabio. The defendant consented to filming jury deliberations, however the District Attorney objected. Judge Poe permitted filming the jury deliberations and allowed the exclusion of any juror who did not wish to be filmed.

Should Judge Poe's opinion be upheld?

Yes:

- ✓ The public has always been free to observe a trial in progress, thus ensuring a free and non secret trial. Similarly, observations of jury deliberations should be permitted.
- ✓ Televising juries is a means of monitoring the workings of government and keeping the system honest. As Harrison's mother stated "The state of Texas wants to kill my son. I think the whole state should be watching."
- ✓ Cameras in the jury room can be educational and potential jurors will know what to expect when called for jury duty.
- ✓ The identity of jurors is always known and there is always a possibility of retaliation whether jury deliberations are televised or not.

No:

- While the public has always been free to observe a trial in progress, the public has never been allowed to view jury deliberations.
- Secret deliberations encourage people to speak freely and share their views. Jurors may be cautious of speaking out if they know they are being judged by a television audience and if they know that their actions and conduct will be subject to post verdict scrutiny. Televised jurors may be reluctant to take an unpopular stand.
- Excluding jurors who do not wish to be televised skews the jury pool.
- In a death penalty case, a juror may be hesitant to impose the death penalty, knowing that the defendant's friends and family members are likely to hold the juror personally responsible for the resulting verdict and may seek retribution.
- Everyone plays to the camera.

Q Should police interrogations be videotaped?

Unreliable confessions are a substantial problem in law enforcement. In 1989 five young men between the ages of 14 to 16 were sentenced to prison for the rape and beating of a woman jogger in Central Park. Their conviction was based upon videotaped confessions made to detectives. Supporters of the five claimed that their statements were coerced. In 2002 the District Attorney recommended dropping all the convictions in the case, citing new DNA evidence that implicated a convicted rapist who subsequently confessed to the crime.

Should all police interrogations be videotaped?

Yes:
- ✓ People are sometimes pressured to confess to crimes they did not commit.
- ✓ Mandatory videotaping of interrogations has been successful in Alaska and Minnesota.
- ✓ Videotaping would more accurately reflect whether confessions were given voluntarily, and thus promote more accurate decision making during the trial.
- ✓ Videotaping entire interrogations will deter police abuse and coercion during interrogations and conversely it will also deter false allegations of coercion.

No:
- Videotaping would make it more difficult to solve crimes.
- Videotaping interrogations would be costly.
- Sometimes statements are made in the field when no cameraman is available.
- Videotaped legal interrogation tactics might appear harsh and shocking to jurors.
- The tapes would have to be edited to eliminate information which juries are not allowed to hear and trials would be lengthened because juries would have to watch the tapes from start to finish.

Related Issue:
Should television cameras be allowed in the courtroom?

Should hate speech be allowed on the internet?

The Council of Europe adopted a measure that would make it illegal to advocate internet hate speech. The amendment bans "any written material, any image or any other representation of ideas or theories, which advocates, promotes or incites hatred, discrimination or violence, against any individual or group of individuals, based on race, color, descent or national or ethnic origin, as well as religion." This measure runs counter to the U.S. Constitution's First Amendment, which guarantees freedom of speech. In the United States, hate speech can be banned only if it is designed to "incite an immediate breach of the peace" or is intended to provoke "imminent lawless action."

Should access to hate speech on the internet be allowed?

Yes:
- ✓ Hate speech in the United States is protected by the First Amendment and receives the same guarantees as any other speech.
- ✓ Global legislation and international cooperation outlawing hate speech is impossible to obtain, because hate speech can be posted lawfully in one country and can be read in other countries where it is unlawful.
- ✓ The internet was created for the free passage of information safe from governmental interference and control.
- ✓ Freedom of expression is more important than the benefits of censorship.
- ✓ Governmental definition of what type of speech is appropriate threatens democracy.
- ✓ The public nature of the internet may work against hate-mongers because their activities can be monitored.
- ✓ Even if the First Amendment to the U.S. Constitution protects hate speech from being prohibited by the government, it does not preclude private companies from restricting what gets posted on their equipment.

No:
- • Hate speech harms its victims and the government has an interest in maintaining order and morality.
- • Speech codes reduce racism.
- • Hate speech is similar to fighting words which incite an immediate violent response and is not protected under the First Amendment.
- • Internet hate sites promote the recruitment of new members into the hate community.

Q   Should free speech be abridged?

Other Issues for Consideration:

Should a magazine article promoting racial hatred be allowed?
Maclean's, a Canadian magazine, published an article by Mark Steyn which denigrated Muslims and depicted Islam as "inhuman and violent." The Canadian Islamic Congress described the article as hate speech. Maclean's argued that publication of the article was part of free speech. In the United States, such speech is constitutionally protected, and in 1997 the American Nazi Party was allowed to march in Skokie, Illinois, despite the many Holocaust survivors living in the area. In other countries however, the promotion of racial hatred could result in fines or imprisonment. Israel and France, for example, forbid the sale of swastikas and other Nazi items, and Holocaust denial is a crime in Canada, Germany, and France.

Should a book or internet site advising that income taxes are voluntary and need not be paid be banned?
Irwin Schiff's book, The Federal Mafia: How The Government Illegally Imposes And Unlawfully Collects Income Taxes advises people that paying income taxes is voluntary and that they are not required to pay any income tax. Federal District Court Judge Lloyd George stated that Mr. Schiff knew that he was offering fraudulent tax advice, and banned the sale and distribution of the book as false commercial speech which is not protected by the First Amendment. Mr. Schiff claimed that his book was political and not commercial, and that prohibiting the book was a violation of his right to free speech.

Should governments restrict internet access?
The Chinese government acknowledged that it restricts access to certain types of online information which it finds to be politically unacceptable, such as govern-mental sites in Taiwan. Should U.S. companies operating in China, such as Google and Microsoft, cooperate with the Chinese government by removing such information from its search engine results?

Should a newspaper publish satirical cartoons of Muhammed?

Should the U.S. release photos of prisoner abuse in Iraq which might "inflame anti-American opinion" by foreign extremists and endanger American lives?

Should a poster depicting a bare-breasted Virgin Mary be withdrawn?

Q Should Iran's President be invited to speak at Columbia University?

Mahmoud Ahmadinejad, the President of Iran, who declared the Holocaust a "myth" and who in public speeches promoted anti-U.S. rhetoric and called for the destruction of the State of Israel, was invited to speak at Columbia University. Following protests on campus, the invitation was cancelled because of security reasons.

Should Mr. Ahmadinejad have been invited to speak at Columbia?

Yes:
- ✓ The university should promote freedom of expression and allow people to express unpopular ideas.
- ✓ Unpopular and repugnant ideas are the cost of free speech.
- ✓ It is possible to learn from those who express unpopular ideas and are critical of our way of thinking.
- ✓ Mr. Ahmadinejad's appearance provides an opportunity to engage him in debate.

No:
- • The university should not provide a platform for hate speech.
- • Mr. Ahmadinejad suppresses academic freedom and free speech in Iran.

Related Issue:
Tariq Ramadan, a Swiss born philosopher, who is the son of Egyptian parents and the grandson of the founder of the Egyptian Brotherhood, is a Muslim intellectual with supposedly radical Islamist views and a fundamentalist political theology. His application for a work visa to teach and lecture at the University of Notre Dame was denied.

Q

Should access to internet pornography be allowed?

The Communications Decency Act (CDA) made it a criminal offense to send indecent material over the internet. The U.S. Supreme Court overturned the law and stated that the act was a violation of the First Amendment.

Should access to pornography via the internet be allowed?

Yes:

- ✓ There is no universal definition of pornography. Because of cultural and legal differences, what may be considered pornographic in one country may not be considered so in another country. The necessary global legislation outlawing pornography would therefore be impossible to obtain.
- ✓ Prohibiting internet pornography is impossible to enforce and impossible to censor.
- ✓ The internet was created for the free passage of information safe from governmental interference and control.
- ✓ Prohibition is a limitation of individual freedom and free speech.
- ✓ Pornographic content is seldom encountered by accident and if you don't like something you don't have to look at it.
- ✓ Parents can use filtering technology to block pornography.
- ✓ Freedom of expression in a democratic society is more important than the benefits of censorship.

No:

- • If pornography is morally offensive, then the majority has a legal right to legislate its regulation.
- • Pornography diminishes the dignity of human life.
- • Pornography frequently condones rape, torture, and violence as a legitimate means of achieving sexual satisfaction and is inappropriate for children.
- • The presentation of live sex acts and other sexual activities via the internet should be restricted.
- • Communication between sexual perverts should not be encouraged.

 **Should access to virtual child pornography be allowed?**

Virtual child pornography uses commercial software to create computer generated fictional images of children, or uses young looking adults, to convey the impression that real children are being depicted, when in fact they are not. Actual child pornography, because it abuses children is subject to a criminal offense, and is not protected by the free speech provisions of the First Amendment.

Should the government while criminalizing actual child pornography allow access to virtual child pornography?

Yes:

✓ Virtual child pornography is a victimless crime. Using actual children in the production of pornography is child abuse, however the element of abuse is absent during the production of virtual child pornography.

✓ Child pornography producers would not risk prosecution for abusing real children if they could legally use computerized images.

✓ Criminalizing virtual child pornography would make the portrayal of a fictional crime illegal. This is a form of thought control which would make the imagination of a crime an actual crime.

✓ Freedom of expression in a democratic society is more important than the benefits of censorship.

No:

• Child pornography is offensive to our moral standards.

• The production and viewing of virtual child pornography could encourage pedophiles, and lead to real child abuse.

• Because it is almost impossible to distinguish a virtual image from a true image, it would be very difficult to prosecute actual child abusers.

• Pedophiles use child pornographic photos to persuade young people that such activity is not unusual.

• Internet use would promote communities of pedophiles.

> Addendum:
> In Ashcroft v. The Free Speech Coalition, the U.S. Supreme Court upheld the legality of virtual child pornography.

Q

Should the contents of your laptop's hard drive be subject to inspection when you enter the U.S.?

In July 2005, Michael Arnold was arrested after arriving in the United States from a vacation in the Philippines. Customs agents inspected his laptop and discovered numerous images depicting child pornography. Arnold was charged with possessing and transporting child pornography, an offense which can carry a 20-year jail penalty. The lower court judge excluded the evidence after finding that customs agents did not have reasonable suspicion to search the contents of his laptop's hard drive. The Appeals Court reversed the decision stating that customs officials did not need reasonable suspicion to search a laptop or other electronic storage device. The ruling however did not clarify whether a traveler has to help the government search his computer by providing log-in information or passwords for encrypted data.

Should U.S. customs be allowed to scrutinize your laptop's hard drive?

Yes:
- ✓ Inspection of a hard drive is no different than inspection of a suitcase.
- ✓ The government has the responsibility of protecting the public.
- ✓ Inspection can thwart terrorist and criminal communications.
- ✓ Pornographers can be arrested as can exporters of illegal technology.
- ✓ Federal employees are prohibited by law to disclose any confidential information which they obtain as part of their official duties.
- ✓ Computer data in hard copy form would be subject to inspection.
- ✓

No:
- The Fourth Amendment prohibits unreasonable searches and reasonable suspicion of a crime should be present prior to any search.
- Your hard drive may contain confidential business plans, tax returns, trade secrets, attorney-client correspondence, and personal medical information.
- Computer memories function as an extension of our own memory capable of storing our thoughts. Presentation of such data may violate the Fifth Amendment right against self incrimination.

> Addendum: In United States v. Arnold, the U.S. Court of Appeals for the Ninth Circuit upheld the right of federal border agents to search a traveler's laptop computer or other electronic device with no requirement of reasonable suspicion. A similar conclusion was reached by the U.S. Court of Appeals for the Fourth Circuit in United States v. Ickes.

Related Issue:
Xuedong Sheldon Meng was sentenced to prison after a U.S. Customs inspection of his computer revealed the presence of export controlled stolen proprietary software programs which he was planning to sell to the Chinese government.

Q Should the government have access to our internet searches?

*A vast amount of highly sensitive personal information is being collected and stored by companies such as banks, credit card companies, phone companies, and even supermarkets. Internet search engines such as Google, Yahoo, AOL, and Microsoft retain a record of the web sites and the search terms which people research online. This information about consumer choices may be extremely valuable to corporations wishing to deliver targeted advertising. The government would also like to obtain this data and examine all search queries in an effort to prevent terrorism. Under the government's **Total Information Awareness (TIA) Program**, the government will collect massive amounts of information on the American public, including but not limited to internet search queries, telephone records, bank records, medical records, airline travel records, library withdrawals, hotel reservations, prescription purchases, school records, and cable television viewing habits. Everyone's personal information and day-to-day transactions, not just those people suspected of a crime or a link to terrorism, would come under government scrutiny in an attempt to profile and identify terrorists.*

Search histories are being used in criminal trials. Robert Petrick was convicted of murdering his wife and dumping her body in a Raleigh, North Carolina lake. Prosecutors brought supporting evidence from his Google internet queries of such terms as "body decomposition", "rigor mortis", "neck", "break", along with topics relating to the depth of the lake where her body was found. The searches were stored on the hard drive of his computer, but the same information could just as easily have been obtained from Google.

Should the government have access to our internet searches?

Yes:
    ✓ Data collection is a powerful analytic tool in the fight against terrorism.
    ✓ The data could also be used to prevent crimes and identify pedophiles.
    ✓ Yes, but the data should be used only in cases where individuals are already under suspicion in criminal investigations.
    ✓ The private sector is already useing such data collection for marketing operations.

No:
    • The program is an assault on our right to privacy. We should be able to search the internet without Big Brother looking over our shoulder.
    • It harbors a tremendous potential for abuse, and searches could be expanded to target religious and racial groups and political opponents.
    • The TIA program monitors everyone and conducts surveillance even when there is no suspicion of wrong doing.
    • It would not be effective in reducing terrorism once terrorists are aware of the extent of the program.
    • Our internet queries are open to misinterpretation.

Q — Should internet cockfight broadcasts be allowed?

Cockfighting is illegal in all fifty states, though it is legal in Puerto Rico. Lawyers for the Advanced Consulting and Marketing Co. which runs a cockfighting web site, are fighting the constitutionality of a 1999 law which criminalizes the sale of depictions of animal cruelty for commercial gain.

Should cockfighting broadcasts be permissible?

Yes:

- ✓ While cockfighting itself may be illegal in all fifty states, broadcasting legal cockfighting is not a crime.
- ✓ Cockfighting is legal in Puerto Rico and in other countries.
- ✓ Cockfighting is part of Puerto Rican tradition and culture, just as bull fighting is part of Spanish culture and boxing is part of American culture.
- ✓ A television station which plays a robbery video is also broadcasting illegal activity.
- ✓ Cockfighting broadcasts should be allowed under the constitutional protection of free speech.

No:

- • Cockfighting is cruel and barbaric and is promoted for entertainment or gambling.
- • The birds have no means of escape, and suffer mutilating injuries.
- • Anti-cockfighting broadcasting laws are similar to laws against child pornography and incitement which are examples of governmental abridgement of free speech.
- • Anti-pornography laws also penalize descriptions of illegal conduct.

Related issue:
Robert J. Stevens, a resident of Virginia, was sentenced to three years in prison for selling videotapes of dog fighting which took place in Japan, where the practice is legal.

Q Should one ever tell a white lie?

A lie is a falsehood uttered with the intention to deceive. A white lie is a harmless lie such as "You look marvelous" or "Your dress is beautiful," where the person making the statement believes it to be false. According to some philosophers there are no circumstances in which one may lie. Others feel that one may lie in certain circumstance such as lying to save a life or lying for the good of those being lied to, for example lying to someone who is terminally ill that he is not terminally ill. The Talmud records a rabbinic discussion between the disciples of Rabbi Hillel and the disciples of Rabbi Shammai concerning how to describe the bride during the wedding festivities. Rabbi Hillel states that in all cases we say that she is beautiful and charming while Rabbi Shammai states that the Bible tells us to distance ourselves from falsehood and we therefore praise her as she is, that is, based on her actual beauty.

Should we tell white lies?

Yes:

    ✓   You may lie at times in order to prevent a terrible wrong.
    ✓   You may lie if it is for the benefit of the person being lied to.
    ✓   In the Bible, when Abraham's wife Sarah learns that she will give birth, she is incredulous, and exclaims that "My master is old." When God tells Abraham what Sarah said, He changes Sarah's words to "I [Sarah] am grown old," in order to save Abraham's feelings.

No:

    •   The more you lie, the greater the chance that lying becomes habitual.
    •   Lies thought to be harmless may not be so.
    •   Lies introduce falsehood into our daily life.

Q Should a lawyer breach confidentiality?

Brian Long, Esq. was advised by his client that at the conclusion of his prison sentence he was going to injure the witness who testified against him during his trial.

Should Mr. Long be required to disclose this confidential information to the police?

Yes:
- ✓ A lawyer should reveal confidential information in order to prevent an act that is likely to result in death, substantial bodily harm, or substantial financial loss to another.

No
- A lawyer's duty is to his client and not to society.
- The obligation of attorney-client confidentiality encourages people to seek legal assistance and to communicate fully and frankly with their lawyer, even as to legally damaging subject matter, thus allowing for proper representation of the client.
- If confidentiality is discretionary, then the lawyer who does not disclose significant information could be held liable, because of the charge that harm could have been prevented had the disclosure been made.

Q

Should reporters be required to reveal confidential anonymous sources of information?

Several reporters face fines or jail sentences for not naming their sources of information. On July 14, 2003 syndicated columnist Robert Novak citing two "senior administration officials" as his sources of information, leaked the identity of Valerie Plame, a covert CIA officer. It is a crime for anyone with access to classified information to disclose the identity of a covert agent. There is speculation that members of the Bush administration leaked the information because Plame's husband contradicted White House claims that Iraq attempted to purchase uranium in Africa.

Should Mr. Novak be required to reveal his source of information?

Yes:

✓ The media may have helped someone (two senior administration officials) violate the law by exposing a secret agent.
✓ The leak may harm national security.
✓ The leak may unjustly harm someone's career and reputation.
✓ A journalist's source of information may help prosecutors and plaintiffs determine the truth, and perhaps bring someone who has committed a crime to justice.

No:

• The flow of valuable and often sensitive sources of information will stop if there is no bond of confidentiality.
• The First Amendment to the Constitution guarantees a free press which is vital to our democracy.
• When you give your word to someone, you have to keep it, despite the possibility of going to jail.
• Leaks often result in better and more accountable government.
• Leaks hinder the government from concealing information from the public.

Related Issue:

Jim Taricani, a television reporter, aired a tape showing an undercover FBI informant in the process of bribing a city official in Providence, Rhode Island. He broke no law by airing the tape, however the court had ordered all those involved (prosecutors, investigators, defendants and their attorneys) not to disseminate any of the tapes. Taricani was convicted of criminal contempt for not revealing who gave him the tape. The judge said that the leak was meant to influence prospective jurors or disrupt the corruption investigation. Should Mr. Taricani be required to name his source of information?

Q

Should warrantless surveillance of U.S. citizens' telephone and e-mail messages by the National Security Agency be allowed?

President Bush authorized warrantless eavesdropping on the international phone calls and e-mails of Americans suspected of having terrorist links.

Should the government be allowed to eavesdrop on international calls and e-mails of American citizens?

Yes:

- ✓ Eavesdropping is a vital and effective tool in the war against terrorism.
- ✓ Further terrorist attacks might be prevented.
- ✓ After 9/11 Congress authorized the President to use military force against terrorists and this implicitly allows listening in on terrorist communications.
- ✓ The President has the duty to collect intelligence data and protect the nation from being attacked.
- ✓ Going to court to obtain warrants restricts quick reactions.
- ✓ Relatively few Americans are targeted.

No:

- The civil rights of Americans are being violated because the government does not have to justify its actions in court.
- The 1978 Foreign Intelligence Surveillance Act states that the government cannot spy on Americans without a court warrant.
- Intelligence information could be obtained through warrants which could be obtained in a secret court up to 72 hours after surveillance has started.

Q

Should a Catholic school teacher be dismissed for signing an abortion rights petition?

Michele Curay-Cramer, an English and Religion teacher at Ursuline Academy, a private Catholic school, was one of many people who signed a full-page ad in the Wilmington Delaware News Journal, endorsing abortion rights. After refusing to retract her public disagreement with fundamental Catholic teaching on abortion, she was fired from her job.

Should Ms. Curay-Cramer have been dismissed from her teaching position?

Yes:
- ✓ Catholic school teachers need to teach students the Catholic faith.
- ✓ The government should not interfere with a religious group's right to choose their own ministers and teachers.
- ✓ Planned Parenthood has a similar right to fire an employee who opposes abortion.
- ✓ It shouldn't matter which doctrines the school chooses to uphold. The school could fire someone for supporting abortion but keep someone who doesn't go to confession or is opposed to capital punishment. It is not the place of the court to decide which beliefs constitute true Catholicism.

No:
- Ms. Curay-Cramer was discriminated against because of her views.
- Other teachers at Ursuline who disagreed with Catholic teaching on other issues, such as capital punishment, had not been similarly punished.
- Doctrinal issues could be used to mask non-doctrinal reasons for employment termination.

Addendum:
A 1978 law forbids employers from discriminating against employees who support abortion rights. U.S. District Judge Kent A. Jordan dismissed Ms. Curay-Cramer's case against Ursuline Academy, ruling that Congress did not intend for the law to apply to a religious school. The U.S. Court of Appeals affirmed the decision.

Related Issue:
Should Michelle McCusker, a non-married pregnant Catholic school teacher, be dismissed because she could not adequately convey Catholic doctrines to her students?

Q

Should DNA samples obtained on the sly without a warrant be admissible in court?

DNA extracted from a cigarette butt thrown away by Rolando Gallego linked him to a bloody towel found at the scene of his aunt's murder in 1993. DNA extracted from a restaurant drinking glass used by Altemio Sanchez linked him to a series of rapes and murders. DNA extracted from saliva on a sealed envelope licked by John Athan linked him to a murder twenty years ago. All of the above DNA samples were obtained surreptitiously, without a court order and without the suspect's knowledge or consent.

Should surreptitious DNA samples be admitted as evidence in court?

Yes:
- ✓ Such collections help police solve crimes.
- ✓ Such collections may eliminate people from suspicion.
- ✓ Judges may deny a request for submitting a DNA sample if there is no reasonable suspicion.
- ✓ Since individuals may legally deny a request to submit a DNA sample, surreptitious collection should be inadmissible.
- ✓ There is no expectation of privacy in discarded trash, cigarette butts, or spittle.

No:
- • Such evidence violates one's constitutional right to privacy and violates the 4th Amendment's protection against unreasonable search and seizure.
- • A warrant should be obtained before any collection of a DNA sample.
- • Police are circumventing the requirement to show probable cause.
- • Innocent people may have their DNA profile stored in a police database.
- • DNA samples give the government a lot of personal information besides identity.

Related issue:
The United States Supreme Court in California v. Greenwood, ruled in 1988, that the Fourth Amendment did not prohibit the search and seizure without a warrant of garbage left for collection at the curb.

Q Should a national DNA data bank be established?

Jane Doe was brutally assaulted in Central Park and DNA collected at the crime scene could not be matched with the limited DNA data base of known felons on file.

Should a national data bank of every citizen's DNA be established?

Yes:

✓ A national DNA data base would be a major tool in solving and reducing crime and in deterring criminals.

✓ It would help identify disaster victims and trace lost or abducted children.

✓ It would allow scientists to increase their knowledge of the role that genes play in disease.

No:

• There will be other uses of a national data base besides solving crimes. For example, DNA analysis might provide information about whether a person or groups of people have a genetic disorder or a predisposition to a disease such as addiction, schizophrenia, or heart disease. Such data in the hands of employers or insurers could lead to refusals of employment and insurance for individuals and racial profiling for other groups of people.

• The data base violates personal privacy and people become research subjects without their consent.

• There will be questions as to which medical research facilities or which drug companies should have access to our personal genetic information and who controls access to the information.

Q

Should cloning be used to produce children?

Reproductive cloning technology is used to create an animal that is genetically identical (has the same nuclear DNA) as another currently or previously living animal. The process involves transferring the nucleus with its DNA from a somatic cell (that is a non sperm or egg cell) into an egg cell of the same species whose nucleus and DNA have been removed. The newly fertilized cell is stimulated to divide and is then transferred to a recipient mother to complete its development. Dr. Hwang Woo Suk of Seoul National University, while opposed to using human cloning technology to produce babies (reproductive cloning), used eggs donated by Korean women and created human embryos by cloning, in order to create stem cell lines which could be used to study and treat disease (therapeutic cloning).

Should humans be cloned?

Yes:

- ✓ Assuming that the risks to mother and child were acceptable, it would enable an infertile couple to have a biologically related child.
- ✓ It would permit reproduction for single people and for same-sex couples.
- ✓ It would allow couples at risk of having children with genetic disease, to have healthy children free of specific diseases.
- ✓ Human cloning could produce genetically identical ideal transplant donors for people in need of an organ transplant.
- ✓ It would allow parents to replace a dead or dying child or relative, with a genetically identical clone.
- ✓ A child's genotype could be pre-selected and individuals with superior traits or special talents and skills could be replicated.
- ✓ Clones will be very different from their genetic twin because they will have grown up in a different environment.
- ✓ Adults have a right to reproduce any way that they can.
- ✓ We would gain knowledge about the nature and degree of genetic determinism.

Should cloning be used to produce children?

No:

- Many cloned animals are born with significant birth defects or may develop defects later in life and die prematurely. Cloning is therefore unethical because of the possibility of inflicting harm on the cloned offspring.
- Human beings are not to be treated as experimental guinea pigs for scientific research.
- Human reproduction would become industrialized and commercialized.
- Cloning might deprive people of their uniqueness and impact mental development.
- By inheriting a genetic identity already possessed by another, there would be great pressures on the emotional development of the child who is trying to establish his or her own identity, particularly if multiples of any single individual were created.
- Cloning may violate a child's "right to an open future."

Related Issues:

Should transgenic animals be created? (For example, pigs which have human genes whose organs might be usable for transplants in humans.)

Should chimeras (animal-human hybrids) be created?

Q Should one be able to bequeath his or her fortune to an animal?

Leona Helmsley, the hotel magnate, left a charitable bequest of close to five to eight billion dollars to be used for the care and welfare of dogs. Needy dogs throughout the country are now celebrating. In addition, she left a $12 million trust fund for the care of her favorite Maltese dog. Her dog's yearly expenses were estimated as follows: a $60,000 guardian fee, $100,000 for security, $8,000 for grooming, $3,000 for miscellaneous expenses, $1,200 for food, and $2,500 to $18,000 for medical care.

Should such a charitable trust be permitted?

Yes:
- ✓ It is her money, and she should have the right to leave her money to whomever she sees fit.
- ✓ Her dog was her best friend.
- ✓ The money could be used to train seeing eye dogs or heroin sniffing dogs.
- ✓ She is in full compliance with all tax laws.

No:
- By giving her estate to a charitable trust, Helmsley avoided a multi-billion dollar estate tax bill, which the government could have used for other worthy purposes. The taxpayer is therefore subsidizing her donation.
- Our tax dollars are "going to the dogs."
- The state should have a greater say on how charitable foundations spend their money.

Addendum:
An individual animal cannot receive a bequest of property because it itself is property. New York and other states permit a pet to be the beneficiary of an "honorary trust" which terminates upon the animal's death or after twenty-one years.

Q Should patients share in the profits from drugs developed from their tissues?

Mr. Jones develops intra-abdominal bleeding in an automobile accident, and urgently requires a splenectomy (removal of his spleen) to stop the bleeding resulting from the trauma. The operation is a success, the bleeding stops, and he returns to work after a normal period of recuperation. A portion of the removed spleen is examined by the pathology department in the hospital and found to be free of any other disease. A researcher in the hospital studies the removed spleen and is able to grow a line of cells which produce a cancer killing chemical. He patents the cell line and is in the process of selling his patent for a large sum of money to a pharmaceutical company when Mr. Jones arrives and sues for a share of the profits.

Should Mr. Jones be able to share in the profits?

Yes:
- ✓ The new drug was developed from his cells and his unique DNA of which he is the exclusive owner.
- ✓ His property rights entitle him to share in the profits.
- ✓ He did not waive his rights with informed consent. In fact he wasn't advised that his spleen would be used for research purposes.
- ✓ He was never informed that economic benefits might result from his tissues.

No:
- • Hospital researchers have always done research on collected specimens in academic medical centers.
- • Mr. Jones made no contribution to growing the new cell line or isolating the new drug.
- • An inability to access these tissues would stifle medical research and future medical progress.

Addendum:
In Moore v. Regents of the University of California, the California Supreme Court ruled that individuals do not retain property rights in their excised tissue.

Related Issue:
Should ethnic groups or groups of patients with the same disease share in the profits from drugs developed from their genetic information?

113

Q Should the all volunteer U.S. army be abandoned?

The all-volunteer army was instituted in July 1973, following years of protest against the draft during the Vietnam war era.

Should the draft be reinstituted?

Yes:

- ✓ The majority of volunteers sign up largely for economic reasons, and the all-volunteer army has been called the "poverty draft", with minorities comprising more than thirty percent of the nation's military.
- ✓ The all-volunteer army is fine in peacetime, however during wartime and during strong economic conditions, it is increasingly difficult for the military to meet its recruitment goals. The military is therefore forced to fill its quotas with less educated recruits such as high school dropouts and those with low IQs.
- ✓ Military service has always been an obligation of citizenship and all citizens have the patriotic duty to defend their country.
- ✓ We can now declare war while risking the lives of very few of the decision makers' children who are not required to serve.
- ✓ The all-volunteer army is not representative of the nation as a whole and most of the population does not bear the burden of war.

No:

- An all-volunteer military creates a corps of professional soldiers who are better motivated, better trained, and more skilled than those soldiers who are drafted.
- Since the turnover rate of volunteers is lower, training costs are therefore also lower.
- The draft is a violation of individual liberty.
- Those who choose military careers do so voluntarily.
- Military service provides an opportunity for self-improvement.

Related Issues:
Should the military recruit foreign mercenaries?

Should the Civil War practice of allowing anyone who was drafted into the military to hire someone else to take his place, or allowing a draftee to pay the government a fee in order not to serve, be adopted?

Should jury duty be voluntary or mandatory?

114

Q Should torture be used during prisoner interrogation?

Five terrorists blow up a school and kill 65 children. Three terrorists are killed during the rescue operation and two are captured alive. There is concern that other terrorists are planning another strike. Similarly, the Associated Press receives a call of a bomb placement. The call is traced and the caller is apprehended (the ticking bomb scenario).

Should torture be used to obtain information to foil another attack or to locate the bomb?

Yes:
- ✓ We need to get information from the terrorist in order to prevent a further attack.
- ✓ Torture can be a successful tool in obtaining information and saving lives.
- ✓ Torture will serve as a means of punishment and as a means of deterrence to others.
- ✓ Federal law should be altered to allow torture in limited instances when authorized by a court-approved "torture warrant" similar to the issuance of a search warrant or a wiretap order.
- ✓ Many countries secretly use torture and violate the Geneva Convention.

No:
- • People will say anything under torture, and needed information will not necessarily be obtained.
- • Information can be obtained with chemically assisted interrogation without resorting to torture.
- • The victims of torture are suspects, and have not been proven guilty.
- • Torture implies that the ends justify the means.
- • Legalizing torture is a step on the path of unchecked government authority and may lead to widespread abuse.
- • Torture is immoral and it degrades humanity and the idea of democracy.

Q Should mandatory retirement regulations be eliminated except in occupations where age is considered important to job responsibilities?

Prof. Jones, a tenured professor of literature, is appealing his university's requirement that he retire at age 65.

Should Prof. Jones be allowed to continue teaching?

Yes:
- ✓ Mandatory retirement is a form of age discrimination and violates the equal protection clause of the Fourteenth Amendment of the Constitution.
- ✓ Self employed individuals are not subject to mandatory retirement and it is unfair to force some members of society to retire at age 65 and allow others to continue working.
- ✓ Age is not a key factor in determining whether you can do your job properly.
- ✓ Older workers possess wisdom that comes only with experience.
- ✓ Rather than punishing those capable individuals who wish to work beyond age sixty five, incompetence can be dealt with on an individual basis.
- ✓ Forcing people to retire increases the economic burden of pensioners on the state.
- ✓ Certain occupational requirements are recognized as legitimate grounds for setting age limits (e.g. fire fighting). A professor who teaches after age 65 is not a hazard to students or society.
- ✓ Placement of younger employees in top positions does not necessarily improve the standards and quality of the profession.

Q **Should mandatory retirement regulations be eliminated except in occupations where age is considered important to job responsibilities?**

No:

- Mandatory retirement opens up positions of employment for younger employees.
- It allows younger employees with new, modern ideas to advance in the professions.
- The age of 65 is chosen as an average age above which people might experience a decline in their mental and physical capacities.
- Mandatory retirement would safeguard society against the detrimental effects that could result from the mistakes or poor judgment of elderly workers.
- Voluntary retirement will not always be sufficient to terminate employment of incompetent elderly workers.

Addendum:

The Age Discrimination in Employment Act of 1967 (ADEA), prohibits employers from using age as a basis for enforcing mandatory retirement. Federal mandatory retirement rules however, apply to several occupational groups, such as airline pilots, air traffic controllers, law enforcement officials, correction officers, and firefighters.

Under Missouri's Constitution, state court judges must retire at age seventy. In Gregory v. Ashcroft, the Supreme Court ruled that Missouri's mandatory retirement of judges does not violate the ADEA.

Should U.S. Supreme Court Justices be appointed for life terms?

Yes:

- ✓ The wisdom that comes only from experience creates a better judge.
- ✓ Life tenure for Supreme Court judges shields them from politics and allows them to act in an apolitical manner in deciding cases.
- ✓ Judges will not have to worry about raising money for re-election campaigns.
- ✓ Judges will not have to worry about displeasing voters with unpopular rulings.
- ✓ Judges will not have to worry about political popularity.

No:

- Physical and mental alertness sometimes diminish with age.
- Life tenure allows judges to remain on the bench when they are no longer doing their best work.
- Voluntary retirement will not always be sufficient to retire an incapacitated judge, and impeachment with its public humiliation will rarely be used.
- Justices time their departures in order to give presidents they like, an opportunity to appoint an ideologically compatible successor.
- Because of medical advances judges are living and serving much longer, and vacancies are less frequent than in the past.
- Older justices may lose touch with the surrounding culture.
- Appointment without possibility of renewal for a fixed term of years, or appointment until a mandatory retirement age would also preserve judicial independence.

Related Issue:
Should judges be elected by popular vote and thus become accountable to the will of the people and responsive to public opinion, or should they be selected by executive appointment or by civil service examinations based on merit?

 **Should people be held responsible for their actions?**

Bobby Joe Long, a convicted serial rapist and murderer, was sentenced to death for his confessed crimes.

Should Mr. Long be held responsible for his heinous crimes?

Yes:
- ✓ As long as people are able to distinguish between right and wrong they should be held responsible for their actions and punished accordingly.
- ✓ People have free will in determining their actions.
- ✓ People try to avoid moral responsibility by invoking determinism.
- ✓ Criminal conduct should not be excused by attributing it to abnormal electrical brain activity.
- ✓ Incarceration is necessary to protect other members of society.

No:
- Functional MRIs have shown that sexual offenders will exhibit abnormal electrical brain activity, and people should not be held accountable for impaired neural activity.
- Mr. Long's brain injury during an earlier motorcycle accident may have contributed to his actions.
- People do not have free will. They do not choose to act immorally. Their actions are predetermined by their uncontrollable genetically determined brain chemistry.

Addendum:
If functional MRIs and PET scans can detect abnormal brain activity and predict violent tendencies, people might be at risk for acts they haven't yet committed. Should these people be monitored?

Q Should parents be responsible and punished for their children's crimes?

Parents are facing substantial lawsuits from victims' families who allege that they should have done more to control their children's activities. Steven Pfiel, who had a history of anti social behavior, was given a hunting knife as a birthday present from his parents for his 17th birthday. Three weeks later he used the knife to murder 13 year old Hilary Norskog. He is now serving a life sentence and Pfiel's parents are being sued by Norskog's mother.

Should parents pay restitution for damages caused by their children?

<u>Yes:</u>
- ✓ Parental punishment provides an incentive for parents to control their children.
- ✓ There are responsibilities to being a parent, and parents must provide adequate oversight.

<u>No:</u>
- Many parents whose children get into trouble have done all they could to control their children.
- One individual should not be held responsible for the crimes of another.
- Children make up their own minds, not only by exposure to their parents, but also by exposure to society in general.

<u>Related Issue:</u>
Should all participants in a crime be responsible for each others' actions? (See felony murder on next page).

Q Should the felony murder rule be repealed?

The felony murder rule holds that any death (even unintended) that occurs during the course of a serious felony such as a burglary, rape, or kidnapping is considered first degree murder and all participants in the felony can be held equally responsible. For example, if someone dies of a heart attack during a robbery, the robber and his getaway driver may both be found guilty of first degree murder.

On March 10, 2003, Ryan Holle lent his car to a friend, knowing that it would be used during a burglary at the home of a marijuana dealer. The dealer's daughter was unintentionally killed during the burglary, and Mr. Holle, although at home during the burglary, was found guilty as an accomplice and sentenced in Florida to life imprisonment without parole.

Should Mr. Holle's sentence be reversed?

Yes:
- ✓ The rule is a miscarriage of justice.
- ✓ The punishment should be proportionate to the degree of culpability.
- ✓ People should be responsible only for their own actions.
- ✓ Intent is not taken into consideration.
- ✓ An accomplice may have disagreed with the other person's action.
- ✓ Premeditation is not taken into consideration.
- ✓ Several states have repealed the rule.

No:
- The rule deters crime because it holds all participants in a felony responsible for the actions of one another.
- A criminal should be considered responsible for all possible consequences of his action.

Addendum:
England abolished the felony murder rule in 1957.

Q Should targeted assassinations (extra-judicial killings) be declared unlawful?

As a general rule, civilians must not be attacked during war. Civilians lose the right to protection under the Geneva Conventions if they directly participate in combat activities.

Israeli helicopters attacked and killed Sheikh Ahmed Yassin, a founding leader of Hamas (listed by the U.S. as a terrorist organization), as he was leaving a mosque in Gaza. Yassin was not directly participating in battle, but the Israelis argue that his participation in the planning and execution of suicide bombings constitutes "direct" participation. Hamas would undoubtedly argue the reverse. Similarly, the United States, as part of the war on terror, fired Predator missiles from a remotely controlled CIA drone, killing Al-Qaeda operatives in Yemen (a non war zone).

Should targeted assassinations be condemned?

Yes:
- ✓ Targeted assassinations are contrary to international law and are a violation of human rights.
- ✓ There is no accountability in anything the government does.
- ✓ People are being killed without trial or due process.
- ✓ At times besides killing the targeted individual, innocent bystanders might be killed.
- ✓ Targeted killing is likely to provoke revenge killings of civilians.
- ✓ Our sense of morals is offended when government officials act like terrorists.

No:

- Hamas is a terrorist organization which has spearheaded a wave of suicide bombings which have killed hundreds of Israeli civilians in the past few years. Every government has the right and the obligation to defend its citizens, and targeted killing of known terrorists is necessary to save innocent lives.
- The "war on terrorism" is not a conventional war as there is no formal declaration of war. The killing of terrorist chiefs who plan and orchestrate murderous attacks and have no reservations about killing innocent civilians is justified.
- Terrorists should not be immune to being targeted and killed. Fighting terrorists cannot be conducted with kid gloves in accordance with pacifist principles.
- Targeting terrorist leaders is legitimate under international law.
- Targeted assassinations are used only when it is not possible to arrest or apprehend the terrorists in question.
- It is ludicrous to describe Ahmed Yassin and Osama bin Laden as non combatant moderate spiritual leaders.

Q **Should the U.S. government limit the outsourcing of jobs to other countries?**

More and more jobs are being outsourced from the United States. The person answering your call to an 800 number may be located in a call center in India. Similarly, computer programmers writing software, lawyers writing research reports, and doctors reading electrocardiograms or x-rays, may be working out of offices in countries located thousands of miles away from the U.S., and being paid salaries much lower than those paid in the U.S.

Should outsourcing be limited by the government?

Yes:
- ✓ By moving jobs overseas, U.S. workers lose employment and income and will find it extremely difficult to find a new job.
- ✓ The loss of these jobs is not creating new jobs in higher paying fields.
- ✓ Those who lose their jobs may have to take lower paying jobs.
- ✓ The loss of jobs reduces the tax base and increases unemployment costs.
- ✓ The cost of government retraining programs will also increase.

No:
- • Moving jobs overseas will save U.S. companies millions of dollars and make them more competitive and more profitable.
- • Outsourcing is good for the American economy.
- • Companies must outsource in order to remain competitive. If we do not outsource, our corporations will be unable to compete in the global economy, and with their collapse, many more jobs will be lost.

Q   Should the prison system be privatized?

Punishment of criminal behavior has traditionally been considered to be a state function. In 1984 the Corrections Corporation of America (CCA) was awarded a contract to run a prison facility in Tennessee. Since that time, private prison management has become a major industry.

Should our prisons be operated by private for profit companies?

Yes:

- ✓ Studies have shown that the private sector can run prisons less expensively and more efficiently.
- ✓ New design and management innovations reduce costs.
- ✓ There is no sacrifice of quality of service.
- ✓ Private management provides relief to cash strapped States trying to cope with the large increases in the number of prisoners.

No:

- Other studies have shown that cost-savings promised by privately managed prisons have not materialized.
- The profit motive could cause management to cut corners, such as hiring uneducated and poorly trained guards, skimping on health care and providing poor and overcrowded conditions.
- Private companies are not interested in rehabilitation to decrease recidivism, as the more prisoners remain incarcerated the more profit for the company.
- Private companies might lobby to increase jail terms, reduce paroles, increase corrections budgets, and exploit the public's fear of crime.

Q Should the U.S. outsource military and intelligence operations to a private military organization?

Blackwater, later renamed Xe Services, is one of several private military companies under contract to the United States government. The company guards officials and military installations and helps in the training of Iraq's army and police. The C.I.A. has hired Blackwater personnel to locate and assassinate top Al Qaeda officials. It is estimated that there are 30,000 to 100,000 armed security contractors working in Iraq.

Should the U.S. government continue to rely on companies like Blackwater?

<u>Yes:</u>

✓ In the absence of a draft, there is no way to secure enough personnel to meet military needs.
✓ Blackwater employees are not mercenaries. They are loyal Americans, who are highly motivated and capable security professionals. Many of them are experienced veterans providing a valuable service to the military.
✓ Blackwater professionals do not engage in offensive missions.
✓ These companies are private security companies providing bodyguards and installation guards. They are not a private army.
✓ Prior to Iraq we had 700,000 contractors during World War II and 80,000 contractors in Vietnam.

<u>No:</u>

• Blackwater employees have been involved in multiple unjustified shooting incidents and have been accused of killing Iraqis without cause.
• Blackwater employees are mercenaries.
• The existence of military companies is a threat to democracy.
• Contractors with the authority to use deadly force raise concerns about legality, oversight, and accountability.
• The Constitution does not permit the establishment of a private army.

125

Q Should English be the official language of the United States?

Contrary to popular belief, the United States has no official language, though English inherited from British colonization is the de facto national language. English is used in treaties and in official governmental pronouncements and one must exhibit a proficiency in English in order to become a naturalized citizen. Over 30 million Americans, however, speak Spanish as a first or second language. Chinese is the third most common language spoken in the United States. California's driving license exam is given in over thirty different languages in order to accommodate its citizens. Bills have been proposed to ban all languages other than English by federal, state, and local governments.

Should English be the official language of the United States?

Yes:
- ✓ The English language is a unifying force among all Americans.
- ✓ English language skills are necessary in order to succeed in the United States.
- ✓ Immigrants cannot find good paying jobs, because of their inability to speak English.
- ✓ English as the official language would promote the learning of English by immigrants.
- ✓ The government will save money by publishing official documents in only one language.
- ✓ Racial conflicts would decrease.
- ✓ Public safety and health needs would be exempt from English-only laws.
- ✓ Bilingual education diminishes the ability of children to learn English.

No:
- • Making English the official U.S. language is anti-immigrant.
- • It overlooks the importance of immigrant culture.
- • Having multiple languages is a great resource for America.
- • Most Americans already speak English.
- • Due process could be violated if courts do not provide translation services.
- • Non English readers may be unable to pass a driver's test written in English.
- • Important communications with non English speaking groups will be impaired.
- • Non English readers might be deprived of their voting rights by English-only ballots.

www.ingramcontent.com/pod-product-compliance
Lightning Source LLC
Chambersburg PA
CBHW072140280526
45788CB00002B/722